How to Write Your Undergraduate Dissertation in Criminology

This book provides a guide for undergraduate criminology and criminal justice students undertaking their final-year dissertation. It speaks to the specific challenges for criminology students who may wish to research closed institutions (such as prisons, courts, or the police) or vulnerable populations (such as people with convictions, victims of crime, or young people), and offers guidance on how to undertake research on these topics while avoiding many of the access and ethical obstacles.

It takes students through each phase of the dissertation, from designing and planning the research to writing up and presenting the completed work. The complexities of undertaking research on sensitive topics and with criminal justice institutions are discussed throughout, offering an insight into some of the challenges that students may be faced with and suggestions to overcome obstacles. It offers practical guidance for empirical and library-based projects and provides students with suggested resources for accessing primary and secondary data. It utilises a mixture of worked examples, top tips, practical strategies, and student activities to ensure the dissertation is a manageable and enjoyable process.

This book will be beneficial to all undergraduate criminology students who have to undertake either a library-based or empirical dissertation. The examples and activities in the book will also be useful for dissertation supervisors who can use them to support their dissertation students.

Suzanne Young is an Associate Professor in Criminal Justice at the School of Law, University of Leeds, UK.

"*How to Write Your Undergraduate Dissertation in Criminology* offers the essential guide to producing your dissertation. From the literature review to the methodology chapter, from finding data to finding your voice, it guides you step by step through the process using examples specific to criminology. As such, it gives you the best chance of excelling in your dissertation."

Dr David Churchill, *Associate Professor in Criminal Justice,*
University of Leeds

"*How to Write Your Undergraduate Dissertation in Criminology* provides a helpful step by step guide to undertaking undergraduate research, complemented by a range of activities to encourage students to think about their dissertation research and writing in a manageable way. This text is also an excellent resource to support teaching and learning on dissertation modules with activities that academic staff can use in their teaching practice."

Dr Helen Nichols, *Associate Professor in Criminology,*
University of Lincoln

"Academic writing is challenging, especially for students faced with writing a dissertation. What is needed is a practical, supportive, and user-friendly guide addressing all stages of the process from selecting a viable topic to producing a final edit. This is that guide. Authored by a leading expert in teaching and learning in criminology, all students will benefit from reading it and putting the advice into action."

Professor Gavin Dingwall, *Professor of Criminal*
Justice Policy, De Montfort University

"*How to Write Your Undergraduate Dissertation in Criminology* will provide students with necessary skills and help them to work with their supervisors to plan and execute a research project. The book is well structured and covers everything students need to know to complete their dissertation. The design of the book is very engaging and encourages students to interact with the content through a series of exercises. As such, it provides an excellent learning resource."

Debbie Jones, *Associate Professor in Criminology, Swansea University*

"This is an excellent, supportive, and engaging book for students embarking on their undergraduate dissertation in criminology. With activities and diagrams to guide decision-making, the book breaks down what can be a daunting task into a manageable – and even enjoyable – process. The practical takeaways make this an essential read for students navigating the dissertation journey."

Dr Christine Haddow, *Lecturer in Criminology,*
Edinburgh Napier University

How to Write Your Undergraduate Dissertation in Criminology

Suzanne Young

Routledge
Taylor & Francis Group

LONDON AND NEW YORK

Cover image: © DKosig / Getty Images

First published 2022
by Routledge
4 Park Square, Milton Park, Abingdon, Oxon OX14 4RN

and by Routledge
605 Third Avenue, New York, NY 10158

Routledge is an imprint of the Taylor & Francis Group, an informa business

British Library Cataloguing-in-Publication Data
A catalogue record for this book is available from the British Library

Library of Congress Cataloging-in-Publication Data
A catalog record has been requested for this book

ISBN: 978-0-367-85998-5 (hbk)
ISBN: 978-0-367-85999-2 (pbk)
ISBN: 978-1-003-01633-5 (ebk)

DOI: 10.4324/9781003016335

Typeset in Bembo
by Newgen Publishing UK

Contents

Illustrations

Figures

Tables

Boxes

Preface

Every year, thousands of undergraduate criminology students embark on their dissertation journey, and every year I would get asked the same questions about the planning and execution of a dissertation. I would encourage engagement with existing dissertation books, but students often reported that they would like a text that spoke directly to them as criminology students. So this text has been inspired by my former students, and I would like to thank those students for offering an insight into what they would find the most useful for guiding them through the dissertation process. To all current and future dissertation students, I hope this text offers you the guidance you need to succeed in your dissertation journey.

What became apparent in writing this text was how important it was for supervisors to be able to use the activities and examples in their own supervision. I have endeavoured to produce a text that students can work through independently, but also one that supervisors can utilise during the supervisory process. I would like to thank the reviewers and my colleagues who offered support and valuable commentary while producing this text (you know who you are) – your advice and suggestions have led to this text being a resource for both students and supervisors. I am entirely grateful for all you have done.

A final word of thanks to Routledge, and specifically Tom and Jessica, who provided endless support and guidance in the production of the text.

Suzanne Young
September 2021

Introduction
How to Use this Book

Well done on reaching the stage in your degree where you get to undertake your own independent research project. Your final-year dissertation is probably the most important piece of work you will complete, largely because it is a representation of the skills and knowledge you have gained on your course. It should also be the proudest piece of work you produce, because it takes dedication and discipline to complete it. The dissertation can be an enjoyable journey, but it also comes with many challenges, so this text has been designed specifically to assist you through the different requirements of your dissertation.

How This Book Can Help

The aim of this book is to assist with the various stages of a dissertation by offering guidance, examples, and activities to help you manage each of the different phases. This text is designed specifically for students studying criminology and criminal justice because there are unique challenges with designing a dissertation that is feasible and ethical when dealing with hard-to-reach populations, closed institutions, and sensitive topics.

This book is structured to take you through each stage of the dissertation, from design and planning to writing and presenting the final piece of work. The book is intended to help you understand the requirements of each stage, no matter whether you are undertaking a library-based or empirical dissertation. The examples and activities included in each of the chapters have been designed for criminology students, with many examples being taken from published undergraduate and postgraduate criminology dissertations.

DOI: 10.4324/9781003016335-1

Table A.I How to Use This Book

Top Tips	These contain tips for helping you with different aspects of a dissertation.
Activities	These are designed to help you applying the guidance in the book to your own project.
Examples	These offer worked examples to illustrate how to undertake different stages in practice.
Tables	These will contain examples and guidance.
Figures and Diagrams	These offer a visual representation of processes.
End of Chapter Checklists	These are included at the end of each chapter to help you stay on track of your progress.

How to Use This Book

This book contains a range of helpful guides, examples, and activities. To ensure you get the most out of the text, these guides and activities have been colour-coded for easy identification. Table I.1 explains how the colour coding can help you easily identify the different features of each chapter.

It is recommended that you work through each chapter of the text according to the different stages and the type of dissertation. The chapters will include activities for you to undertake, and there is a checklist at the end of each chapter to help you keep organised throughout the process. There is suggested further reading at the end of each chapter to signpost you to additional reading you should undertake to complement this text.

Finally

If you are having any doubts about your ability to undertake a dissertation, remember this: *You are good enough to have gotten to this stage of your degree, so you are good enough to see it through to the end.*

Chapter 1

What Is a Dissertation?

Overview

Undertaking a dissertation for the first time can be a daunting task for any student. The first step in writing a dissertation is ensuring you understand what a dissertation is, and what is expected of you. This chapter will discuss the aims of a dissertation, the role of your supervisors, and the processes involved in completing a dissertation.

By the end of this chapter, you should be confident in understanding:

- The purpose of a criminology dissertation
- The different types of dissertations in criminology
- The complexities of undertaking a dissertation in criminology
- What a dissertation should comprise

Aims of a Dissertation

A dissertation is a research project undertaken as part of your undergraduate degree. It is an **independent** piece of work that is designed by you and focuses on one specialist topic. The purpose of a dissertation is to showcase the accumulation of skills and knowledge you have gained during your degree. These skills include independent study, sourcing information, formulating a research question, data collection, critical analysis, and independent thinking. A dissertation is unlike an essay, not only due to the length (unlike an essay, a dissertation can range from 8000 to 12000 words in length, depending on your institution) but also in the task. Unlike essays, where you are set a question to answer, dissertations require you to choose the topic and devise your own questions to be researched. The dissertation is a demonstration of

DOI: 10.4324/9781003016335-2

you being able to work truly independently by developing your **own ideas** through a critical analysis of evidence on a specific topic.

The requirements of a dissertation in criminology are as follows:

- You identify an issue that requires investigation
- You undertake in-depth systematic reviews of the existing literature on that topic
- You formulate a feasible research question that you can answer
- You devise a strategy for collecting information to answer your research question
- You critically analyse the information you have gathered
- You draw conclusions from the analysis

A dissertation is more than just a demonstration of knowledge; it is a **validation** of what you research and why. In other words, you need to ensure that the research question serves a purpose and that the methods you choose will be the most appropriate to answer your question. Therefore, it is equally important in a dissertation to evidence the process by justifying your decisions. Each stage of your dissertation ought to be validated in the following ways:

- Justify the focus of your dissertation: why have you chosen to research that topic?
- Justify your research questions: why are you asking those questions, and why are they important?
- Justify your data collection strategy: why have your chosen one method over another?
- Justify your analysis: why have you chosen to analyse the data the way you have?

Dissertations should also demonstrate a level of **originality** – there would be little point in researching something that we already know the answer to – however, you are not expected to produce groundbreaking new work in the field. Originality means contributing something new by **building on** previous knowledge and/or methods. Your dissertation can be original in different ways, whether it be in the application of theory, the choice of method, or the development of new arguments. As Greetham (2014: 12) states:

> Remember, you don't have to show that what you plan to do has never been done before. In many cases what's original is that

you have done it for yourself, rather than rely on other people's research.

This may all sound daunting at this stage, but that is only because you have not done it before. You have already developed the skills required for the dissertation throughout the duration of your course; the dissertation is just a means of showcasing them. So, let us now consider the different stages involved in undertaking a dissertation.

The Role of Your Supervisor

As part of your dissertation, you will be allocated a supervisor, who will most likely be a member of staff in your school/department. Supervisors play a crucial role in supporting you during the dissertation process, so it is important that you understand the supervisory relationship. Your own course will have set out the core duties of your supervisor and the time given to supervision, so it is advisable to familiarise yourself with the supervisory requirements in your own institution. While there are different models of supervision depending on your own department, supervisors generally act as academic facilitators, and their role normally includes:

- Ensuring you understand the requirements for a dissertation
- Offering guidance on planning a viable dissertation project
- Meeting with you to discuss your progress and plans
- Directing you to resources to help you through the dissertation process
- Ensuring you abide by any ethical requirements
- Helping to keep you on track at the different stages of the dissertation
- Providing feedback on your progress
- Offering support during times when you might feel lost in the dissertation process

Supervisors will be there to keep you calm, keep you on track, and offer guidance and support throughout. Remember that the dissertation is an independent piece of work, and thus your supervisor should not be expected to design your dissertation for you. Unlike in other coursework where questions and topics are set for you, the dissertation requires you to set these yourself, and your supervisor will help you in this process. Supervisors can also be vital in helping you present your dissertation according to the regulations set out on your course. They want to see you reach your potential and produce work of the highest quality; therefore it is advisable to develop a good working relationship with your supervisor. Box 1.1 offers some top tips on how to do this.

Box 1.1 Top Tips: Working With Your Supervisor

1 Attend any supervisory meetings
2 Complete tasks set by your supervisor
3 Keep supervisors up to date with your progress
4 Advise supervisors of any difficulties you are having
5 Don't be afraid to ask your supervisor questions

Dissertation supervision will take different forms depending on your institution and your individual supervisor. It will most likely involve regular meetings during the dissertation process whereby you can update your supervisor on your progress and discuss any issues or challenges you are facing. It is therefore essential that you attend any meetings set by your supervisor to gain the most benefit from their guidance. If your supervisor sets you a task to complete or asks you to submit a piece of work, then it is advisable you do as they request. Tasks are set to help you through the dissertation and are there for your benefit; they also provide valuable opportunities for feedback on your work. At times there may be long gaps between your supervision meetings, but it is important to keep your supervisor updated with how things are progressing, especially if you have faced obstacles. Supervisors have a wealth of experience in both supervising student dissertations and undertaking their own research, and this makes them best placed to answer queries you have. Do not be afraid to ask for help, whatever questions you have; your supervisor will be more than happy to answer them and help you move forward.

Types of Dissertations in Criminology

There are different ways to approach a dissertation, which might seem confusing at first, but the type of dissertation you produce will very much depend on what your research question is and what data is available to you. Broadly speaking, there are two types of dissertations in criminology: the empirical dissertation and the library-based dissertation. Each of these will be discussed in turn. It is important to note that neither type of dissertation is easier than the other; both require the same level of planning, critical analysis, and originality.

Library-Based Dissertations

A library-based dissertation is one that relies solely on previous theory and research to answer a research question. A library-based project requires you to develop a research question that can best be answered using existing material, and this material is what you critically analyse to answer your research question. The advantages of doing a library-based dissertation are that there are very few ethical constraints (unless you are accessing materials that are not freely available in the public domain) and logistically it is easier to use existing sources than to create new ones. This type of dissertation is more than simply summarising the work of others; it requires careful planning, resourcing, and the development of critical arguments. A library-based piece of work involves gathering a large body of existing literature and undertaking in-depth critical analysis of arguments and evidence. This piece of work will be **grounded in theory** with the application of theoretical frameworks and theoretical concepts. You are then tasked with developing your own line of arguments based on that analysis and will need to justify your arguments with relevant readily available evidence. In this type of work, it is important that the research question you aim to answer is not one to which we already know the answer, otherwise your dissertation will lack originality. If undertaking a library-based dissertation, you will need to consider how you will explore literature in a new way, which may involve the application of a different theoretical perspective, exploring relationships between existing literature, or the inclusion of different disciplines of knowledge.

Empirical Dissertations

An empirical dissertation is one that requires you to collect and analyse your own data or undertake secondary analysis of existing data to answer your research question, where your question cannot be answered using existing literature. Empirical dissertations are advantageous because they allow you to explore a topic in a new way and offer you the opportunity to collect and analyse your own data, and you can add new data to the field of study. Empirical dissertations require careful planning to ensure the research is ethical, achievable within the timeframe, and suitable for the level of research training you have had. In designing an empirical study, you need to consider your epistemological perspective, sampling strategy, data collection methods, and approach to data analysis. You are then tasked with drawing conclusions from your data, discussing these in relation to existing research, and identifying the contribution of your data. In this type of dissertation, it is important to set realistic research questions that can be answered with a practical mode of data collection.

Complexities of Criminology Dissertations

The discipline of criminology is unique in that it takes an interdisciplinary approach to exploring crime, criminal justice, and victimisation. The prospect of being able to undertake a piece of independent research on crime is appealing for students, but it also makes dissertations more complex. The nature of the discipline means there are **strict ethical and access limitations** that need to be considered before you can even begin designing a study for investigation. All universities will have rigorous ethical procedures for undergraduate dissertations, and you should make yourself familiar with these at the start of your dissertation process. Table 1.1 lists some common areas of interest for dissertation students and the difficulties undertaking empirical research. The complexities largely relate to ethical issues, but access, time restrictions, and experience of the researcher can all be barriers to undertaking research with certain populations.

The complexities outlined in Table 1.1 need to be considered at the outset of the dissertation process. I recommended you read the British Society of Criminology's Statement of Ethics thoroughly to ensure you are familiar with your responsibilities as a researcher if you intend to undertake research with human participants. Further discussions of access and ethics for criminology topics are covered in Chapter 3 of this text.

Table 1.1 Complexities of Criminology Dissertations

Area of Interest	Complexities
Criminal justice institutions, e.g. • Police • Probation • Prisons • Courts	• Accessing these institutions can be very difficult and time consuming. • You will likely need to negotiate access with gatekeepers. • You may be required to undergo security clearance and/or training. • Closed institutions, such as prisons, will have their own ethical review processes before research access can be granted.

Area of Interest	Complexities
Victims of crime	• Researching crime victimisation is considered a sensitive topic. • Researching people who have been victimised can lead to additional trauma. • Research of this kind should only be undertaken by highly experienced researchers.
Persons considered vulnerable e.g. • Homeless • Cognitive impairments • Under 16 years old • Mental illness	• Research with people who can be considered vulnerable is normally not suitable for undergraduate dissertations. • The priority of the researcher is the wellbeing of participants; this includes their physical and psychological wellbeing. • Individuals under 16 would require parental/guardian consent.
People involved in criminal activity	• You need to consider what your limits to confidentiality will be from the outset. • You are required by law to report to the authorities any information relating to acts of terrorism, money laundering, or neglect or abuse of a child.
Cybercrime	• You need to be aware of the boundaries between what is public and what is private. • There are differences in the data protection laws across different jurisdictions.

There are many topics in criminology that are best suited to a library-based approach. Listed below are some examples of research areas where a library-based approach might be more appropriate due to the nature of the topic, the characteristics of a sample, or the difficulties in accessing original data:

• Undertaking research into a closed institution
• Undertaking research on young people under the age of 16
• Undertaking research that requires international travel
• Undertaking research with people who are considered vulnerable
• Undertaking research on topics that are considered sensitive
• Undertaking a theoretical piece of research

Chapters 2 and 3 of this text will provide guidance on how to assess whether a project is best suited to an empirical or a library-based approach.

Stages of a Dissertation

Managing a large project can be made easier by breaking it down into stages. There are different stages to a dissertation, which have been illustrated in Figure 1.1. Each stage of the dissertation will vary in length, but generally, the dissertation can be split up into three key stages no matter what type of dissertation you undertake:

1 Planning and preparation
2 Data collection and analysis
3 Writing up and drawing conclusions

Each stage of the dissertation will evaluate different skills, including designing a project, identifying and locating sources, applying theory, collecting relevant data, interpreting information, and developing critical arguments. It is therefore important that you allocate time equally to the various stages.

It should be evident from Figure 1.1 that the design stage of the dissertation requires careful planning and consideration. Developing a viable research question takes time, and devising effective methods to answer the proposed question will be central to ensuring the remainder of the research process is a success. I recommend that equal time be dedicated to all three stages of the dissertation to ensure a well-thought-out and achievable project. This book will guide you through each of the stages by offering practical advice in each chapter.

What an Undergraduate Dissertation Looks Like

Many students find it helpful to know what a dissertation looks like before they commence their own. Your own institution may have example dissertations to look at, and I recommend you do this. The *Internet Journal of Criminology* is a useful resource for exploring example dissertations. It publishes undergraduate and master's dissertations that have achieved a first-class mark; as you look through these, you will see variations in the structure and layout of the dissertations which are determined by the type of dissertations and the requirements set out by different institutions.

Dissertations, unlike essays, are set out in chapters (much like a book), with each chapter representing a different section of the dissertation. The structure of chapters will be dependent on the type of dissertation you undertake. The contents of the different sections of a

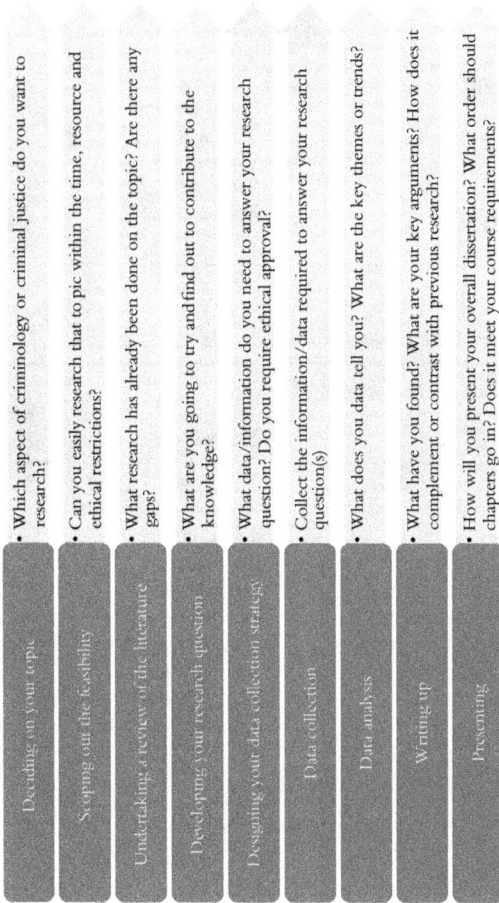

Figure 1.1 Stages of a Dissertation.

Deciding on your topic
- Which aspect of criminology or criminal justice do you want to research?

Scoping out the feasibility
- Can you easily research that to pic within the time, resource and ethical restrictions?

Undertaking a review of the literature
- What research has already been done on the topic? Are there any gaps?

Developing your research question
- What are you going to try and find out to contribute to the knowledge?

Designing your data collection strategy
- What data/information do you need to answer your research question? Do you require ethical approval?

Data collection
- Collect the information/data required to answer your research question(s)

Data analysis
- What does you data tell you? What are the key themes or trends?

Writing up
- What have you found? What are your key arguments? How does it complement or contrast with previous research?

Presenting
- How will you present your overall dissertation? What order should chapters go in? Does it meet your course requirements?

Table 1.2 Empirical Dissertation Example Structures

Empirical Dissertation Example Structures	
Example 1	*Example 2*
Title page	Title page
Acknowledgements	Acknowledgements
Abstract	Abstract
Introduction	Introduction
Literature Review	Literature Review
Methodology	Methodology
Findings	Discussion of Findings
Discussion	Conclusion
Conclusion	Reference List
Reference List	Appendices
Appendices	

Table 1.3 Library-Based Dissertation Example Structures

Library-Based Dissertation Example Structures	
Example 1	*Example 2*
Title page	Title page
Acknowledgements	Acknowledgements
Abstract	Abstract
Introduction	Introduction
Literature review	Methodology
Theoretical framework	Literature review
Analytical writing (2–3 chapters)	Analytical writing (2–3 chapters)
Conclusion	Conclusion
Reference list	Reference list
Appendices	Appendices

dissertation will be covered in more depth in the subsequent chapters, but you can expect that your dissertation will eventually follow a structure like those suggested in Tables 1.2 and 1.3.

Preparing for Your Dissertation

A good way to ease any uncertainty or concerns about undertaking a dissertation is to ensure that you are prepared. You will most likely be provided with **introductory materials** such as module guides at the start of your dissertation, and I recommend you read these through carefully to make sure you understand your institution's format and requirements for the dissertation.

A further recommendation is that you devise a time management plan from the outset. One of the main obstacles students can face when undertaking a large piece of independent work is managing their time effectively. Remember that you will most likely have other modules to study at the same time as preparing your dissertation, and it is **your**

Box 1.2 Student Activity 1

Activity 1: Create a Timetable

Create your own bespoke timetable to help you manage your time. Remember to include rests and time for yourself.

- Step 1: Create a table that lists the days and times of the week, like the blank one below
- Step 2: Note down everything you must do each day (include all your commitments, such as classes to attend, preparatory work for modules, social activities, time to relax, time with family/ friends, work and volunteering commitments, and so on)
- Step 3: Reflect on the days/times you know you work best; there's no point scheduling yourself to do work in the evenings if you don't work well at that time
- Step 4: Schedule yourself time to work on your dissertation on the days/times you are free and will work most effectively

	Monday	Tuesday	Wednesday	Thursday	Friday	Saturday	Sunday
8:00							
9:00							
10:00							
11:00							
12:00							
13:00							
14:00							
15:00							
16:00							
17:00							
18:00							
19:00							

responsibility to schedule time every week to make progress on your dissertation. It is suggested that you create a bespoke weekly, biweekly, or monthly timetable so you note the days and times when you can feasibly work on your dissertation. Complete the activity in Box 1.2 to help you start managing your time from the start.

The dissertation is a large piece of work that requires not only good time management skills but also effective organisation skills. Throughout the dissertation process you will be collecting information, taking notes, developing ideas, and making cross references between literature and evidence. It is advisable to create a **dissertation diary**. A research diary enables you to keep a note of your progress, jot down ideas, detail the different stages you undertook, and write down your reflections. The diary will be helpful for keeping key information in one place and can be particularly helpful for writing your methodology chapter (see Chapter 7). It is also useful for reflexive writing as you keep a record of how the dissertation is progressing, and at what points you faced obstacles. Try to create your own dissertation diary using the activity in Box 1.3.

Box 1.3 Student Activity 2

Activity 2: Create a Dissertation Diary

A dissertation diary can be useful for keeping track of your progress and noting down what you did and when. This can be used for both library-based and empirical projects.

A research diary can include:

- Developing your ideas for your project
- Dates/timeframes of when you undertook work on your dissertation (sourcing literature, collecting and analysing data, writing up, etc.)
- Details of the different stages of designing, undertaking, and completing the dissertation
- Personal thoughts and reflections on how the dissertation is going at the different stages
- Notes or ideas you have during the dissertation
- Questions to ask yourself or come back to in the dissertation

You could create an electronic or paper research diary; it just needs to be a system that keeps all your information organised in an accessible way.

Summary and Checklist

You should now be aware of the aims and expectations of an undergraduate dissertation in criminology. This chapter has offered guidance on preparing for your dissertation and what you should expect from the process. Before moving on to the next chapter, complete the checklist in Box 1.4.

Box 1.4 Checklist

1 Understood the requirements set out by your course/institution ☐
2 Read your course/institution's ethical requirements ☐
3 Gained an understanding of the role of your supervisor ☐
4 Looked at some example dissertations ☐
5 Completed activities 1 and 2 of this chapter ☐

Further Reading

Read your department's dissertation guidance/dissertation handbook to ensure you understand the requirements for your dissertation, wherever you are studying.

Burnett, J. (2009) *Doing Your Social Science Dissertation*. London: Sage, Chapters 1 and 2.

Smith, K., Todd, M. and Waldman, J. (2009) *Doing your Undergraduate Social Science Dissertation*. London: Routledge, Chapter 1.

Chapter 2

Designing Your Criminology Dissertation

Overview

This chapter will take you through the key stages of designing a dissertation. The chapter commences with common mistakes made by students when designing a dissertation, providing example scenarios. It will cover what is meant by research questions, how to design research questions, and how to ensure your questions are realistic and answerable. The chapter will move to discussing the relationship between research questions and research methods, which is crucial to ensuring a well-designed piece of research.

By the end of this chapter you should:

- Be able to avoid unrealistic/problematic dissertation topics
- Understand how to design a suitable research question
- Understand the relationship between research questions and research methods

Problematic Criminology Dissertation Proposals

Students routinely commence their dissertation planning with problematic proposals that are often a result of their personal experience, their connections with individuals and organisations, and their lack of awareness of ethical issues. To ensure you do not propose a problematic topic, undertake the Activity in Box 2.1.

DOI: 10.4324/9781003016335-3

Box 2.1   Student Activity 3

Activity 3: Identify the problems with these proposals

Read through each scenario and note down why you think it is problematic.

Scenario 1

Leslie wants to do a research project in a local prison. She has been volunteering there for six months and wants to interview some of the prisoners for her dissertation. She believes that, because she has been a volunteer, access will not be problematic.

Scenario 2

Charlie is interested in gangs and wants to explore factors that lead young people to joining gangs. She knows of local gangs in her hometown and wants to undertake focus groups with gang members, some of whom she went to school with. Charlie is confident that because she knows these individuals personally, it will be easy to get them to participate.

Scenario 3

Ali wants to research support offered to victims of crime. He works at Victim Support and has discussed the idea with some colleagues who said they would find the research of interest. He has the contact details of victims who could be invited to participate. Ali intends to undertake qualitative interviews with participants to get an in-depth understanding of their experiences.

Scenario 4

Chrissy has designed a qualitative study to understand crime prevention measures in urban and rural communities. She plans to sample six communities, undertaking two focus groups (made up of five people) in each and asking participants to take part in follow-up semi-structured interviews.

In scenario 1, the student has not considered the practical or ethical issues involved in undertaking prison research. All research in a prison requires security clearance and/or training and ethical clearance from the HMPPS National Research Committee. Volunteering or working in a prison does not entitle anyone to carry out research there. For further discussions of undertaking research in prison, see King and Liebling (2007), Liebling (1999), and Martin (2000).

In scenario 2, the student has not considered the potential harm to both herself and the participants in undertaking research of this kind. Empirical research with people who identify as gang members is problematic for even the most experienced researchers. They are considered a hard-to-reach population due to the illegal activities they undertake, and this is often an explanation for the scarcity of research with gang members (see Pawelz, 2017). Research of this type has ethical and legal implications for both researcher and participants and therefore should be avoided as an undergraduate project.

In scenario 3, the student is assuming that because they work in an organisation that supports their idea, they will be able to undertake the project. Even in a situation like this, the student is proposing to conduct research with a group considered vulnerable. Discussing people's victimisation can be very traumatic and can lead to secondary victimisation. Protecting participants from harm is an ethical obligation, and any research that could jeopardise that should be avoided. It is essential that any proposed research is considered ethical by your institution in the first instance, and only then should you approach organisations. For further reading on the complexities of researching victims, please see Walklate (2007).

Finally, in scenario 4, Chrissy's study is too ambitious for an undergraduate project. Undertaking 12 focus groups and potentially up to 60 interviews is unmanageable; the fieldwork alone for this type of project could take 6–12 months. Chrissy would need to reduce the scope to ensure it is feasible. Reducing the number of focus groups and not undertaking interviews would ensure the project is manageable.

There are further access and ethical issues with scenarios 1–3 which are discussed in more detail in Chapter 3 of this text. The remainder of this chapter will take you through the different steps to help you develop a feasible dissertation topic.

Choosing Your Dissertation Topic

Choosing your dissertation topic can seem daunting at first, and many students do not know where to start. This stage of the dissertation planning should not be rushed; it is expected that you will take time to pick a topic to avoid necessary changes later. Box 2.2 offers some dos and don'ts of choosing your topic, which is a good place to start.

Box 2.2 Top Tips: Choosing Your Topic

Things you should do:

- Choose a topic that you have enjoyed learning about to date
- Choose a relevant topic, something that is contemporary
- Choose a topic where there is existing literature to draw on

Some things to avoid:

- Topics you have no knowledge on; they will only give you more background work to undertake
- Choosing a topic simply because you have connections to individuals or organisations
- Topics that have limited or no existing research/literature. Ask yourself why that might be the case – sometimes a gap in research is there for a reason

---

Picking that initial topic can be difficult, but there are simple steps you can follow, and the example in Box 2.3 illustrates how this can be done. Some steps to consider when choosing your topic are:
Step 1: Identify potential topics

- Choose a topic you are interested in
- Reflect on what modules/lectures/readings you have enjoyed on your course to date
- Write down any topics you are not interested in
- From the topics you are interested in, try to shortlist your top two or three

Step 2: Narrow it down to one topic

- Read some introductory material on your shortlisted topics
- Ask yourself what readings keep you most engaged. Which did you want to read more about?
- Reflect on why you find the topic so interesting; this should help you rule out the other topics

---

Box 2.3 Worked Example of Choosing Between Topics

Ayesha is struggling to pick the broad topic for a dissertation. She looks back over the modules and lectures from the past two years and makes a list of all the topics she enjoyed and the ones she enjoyed least. The two topics she was most drawn to in her previous modules and assignments are the policing module and the assignments she wrote on substance misuse (step 1 complete). Ayesha is having difficult choosing between the two, so she takes a proactive approach to explore both topics in more detail. She starts off with an introductory book on policing and an introductory book on drugs and crime. After reading through these books, she realises that she found herself being more drawn into the book on policing than the one on substance misuse and becomes confident she should do a dissertation on something related to policing (step 2 complete).

Ayesha scopes out whether there are past dissertations on policing and notices that there is a variety of empirical and library-based dissertations that have explored different aspects of policing, so she becomes confident that she can design a research project in the field of policing.

Narrowing Down Your Dissertation Topic

Once you have decided on your broad topic, you are now ready to begin the process of narrowing down your topic and devising a suitable research question. A flow chart has been provided in Figure 2.1 to illustrate the steps you need to undertake to develop a suitable research question. This section will discuss how to work through each of the stages.

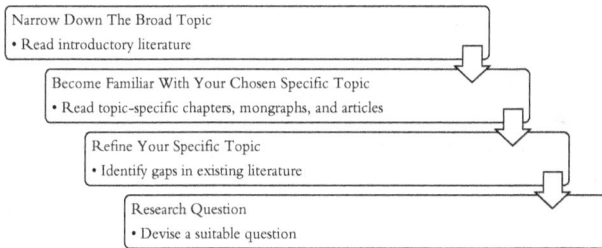

Figure 2.1 Narrowing Down Your Topic.

Once you have established your broad topic area, you should begin to identify the possible areas of investigation. This can be done by skimming over introductory texts in your chosen topic. From the initial skimming of literature, you want to determine what strands of the topic you are most interested in. This should lead you on to reading more specific texts, chapters and journal articles in the topic area. The next step is to explore what research has already been undertaken on your chosen topic and note down any gaps (see Box 2.4).

Box 2.4 What Does Finding a Gap Mean?

When we talk about a "a gap" in research, we mean something we do not already know or something that has not been done in a particular way before. It does not mean that any new research has to be entirely ground-breaking.

You can identify much smaller gaps in research that are more achievable for an undergraduate project. Some suggestions are:

- Applying a different theoretical framework
- Applying a different method
- Looking at different socio-demographic groups
- Drawing on more contemporary resources

A worked example has been provided in Box 2.5 to demonstrate how to narrow down a topic to a specific focus. Narrowing down a topic requires patience and willingness to become familiar with the literature in an area. This step takes time in the planning process and is essential to devise a suitable question, as illustrated in the example in

Box 2.5: the student had to explore all the avenues of a topic before being able to narrow it down effectively. To identify areas of the topic with less research, he had to read widely to establish what research had and had not been undertaken.

Undertaking this volume of reading in the early stage may seem time-consuming, but it will benefit you in the long term. Becoming familiar with the topic at the early stages will ensure that your dissertation is grounded in existing literature, which will make it relevant and contemporary. The reading will also help you identify key readings for dissertation chapters that you will write in the later stages.

Box 2.5 Example of Narrowing Down a Topic

Jai has decided that he would like to undertake research on the topic of ethnicity and crime, which is a very broad topic.

- Jai begins by reading a textbook on ethnicity and crime and notes down all the different topics within the text
- From the reading, Jai decides he is most interested in policing ethnic minority communities
- Jai reads specific articles and book chapters on policing ethnic minority communities
- Jai finds his interest lies mainly in arrest decisions by the police and how these differ between different ethnic minority groups
- Jai notes from the reading that there is less research specifically exploring the police arrest decisions with regard to young black women

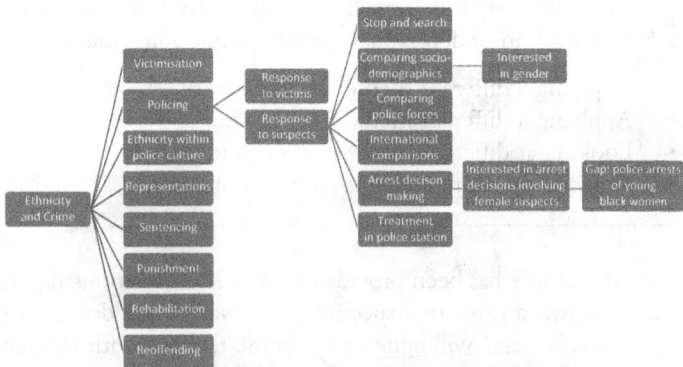

Devising Your Research Question

It is often the case that once students have narrowed down their topic, they struggle to design an actual research question. This can be frustrating, but it is entirely normal. **The research question** is what you are going to address in the dissertation and will guide the type of dissertation you undertake and the type of data you will collect. Devising a good question is important to ensure your dissertation is coherent, focused, and achievable. When designing your research question, make sure it meets the following criteria:

- **Clear**: Research questions should be comprehensible to a lay reader. Avoid the temptation to develop an overly complex research question.
- **Specific**: A vague question will be difficult to answer. The question needs to be specific so it can direct you to a focused method of data collection and analysis.
- **Relevant**: Research questions should arise from issues raised in the literature that you have read.
- **Purposeful**: There needs to be a reason why you are asking a question. It may be to contribute to academic knowledge, address a policy issue, test a theory, or evaluate practices.
- **Manageable**: You need to be able to answer the question with the time, resources, and data available to you.
- **Original**: The question should come from your ideas and initiative. You should not copy questions from other projects or pieces of work. You should also not pose a question we already know the answer to.
- **Interesting**: It should be a question that sparks intrigue, one that will keep you interested and one that will be of interest to your readers.

Now that you know the requirements of a good question, can you spot what is problematic with the questions in Box 2.6?

Box 2.7 provides examples of good research questions, with explanations about why they work particularly well for undergraduate dissertations. Each of the example questions meets the criteria set out above.

Box 2.6 Student Activity 4

Activity 4: Spot the Problems with These Questions

Can you identify what is problematic with the following example research questions using the criteria?

1 Why do people commit crime?
2 Has youth crime changed over time?
3 Has news reporting of Brexit changed people's views of immigration?
4 Are black men disproportionately stopped and searched by London Metropolitan Police officers?
5 Why do the public like movies about serial killers?
6 What impact has austerity had on policing?

Box 2.7 Examples of Good Research Questions

1   What are the main challenges facing police officers in South Yorkshire in tackling car theft?

This is a good question because the purpose of the question is clear. It has a specific focus on one police force and on one type of criminal behaviour. The question is purposeful as the data could be used to help inform strategies to reduce car theft. This is a manageable project and could be undertaken using either a survey, a focus group, or interviews.

2   Did the newspaper reporting of the 2017 Manchester Arena bombing differ between local and national newspapers?

This is a good question because it is very clear and concise. It plainly states the research is on one type of media – newspapers – and the coverage of one specific event. The question will provide an interesting insight into whether there are differences in reporting, considering the different agendas of national and local newspapers.

3   To what extent does the mitigating factor of "sole or primary carer for dependent relatives" reduce sentence severity for women?

This question has a core purpose: to explore factors that affect sentencing. To avoid this topic being too broad, the question is only focusing on one mitigating factor and only focusing on women. This ensures the project is manageable and original. The research will offer an insight into sentencing decisions, making it purposeful and interesting.

4   Can subcultural theory be applied to understanding knife crime in the UK?

This question has an explicit focus, it is starting out with a theoretical framework, and it will explore whether the theory can help explain a particular crime (in this case, knife crime). This is a manageable question as it will be drawing on existing literature and studies relating to knife crime. It is also interesting because it will offer an insight into the extent to which culture plays a role in explaining this type of behaviour, which has been deemed as a contemporary issue.

Once you have your defined topic, you will want to brainstorm different questions that would be worth asking, using the criteria set out above ('Devising Your Research Question') as a guide. If we take the example in Box 2.5, the student, Jai, has decided on his topic and the next stage is to devise a suitable question. Jai brainstorms three possible questions (see Figure 2.2). The first question is slightly vague, which would make the data collection and analysis more difficult; there might also be problems with recruiting a suitable sample. The second question is more focused; however, the available literature and data already show that black women are twice as likely to be arrested than white women. The third question expands on the second to look specifically at the younger age group. There is available data on police arrests broken down by gender, age, and ethnicity, so Jai could use this to run his own analysis. Jai chooses question three as it meets all the criteria needed for a good question.

Brainstorming different questions and considering whether they are suitable based on ethics, time, resources, and originality will provide you with the opportunities to explore different avenues before

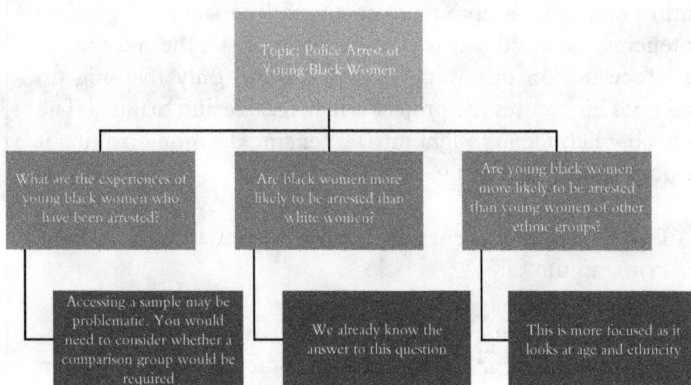

Figure 2.2 Brainstorming Research Questions.

you devise your final question. When considering possible research questions, ask yourself these four questions:

- Has the question already been answered in existing literature?
- Will it be possible to collect the data needed to answer the question?
- Is it a worthwhile question with a clear purpose?
- Is the question manageable?

Types of Research Questions

When brainstorming your questions, you may want to consider the different types of questions that researchers often ask. The type of question you choose will determine the type of dissertation you undertake, the methodological approach needed to answer it, the type of data you need to collect, and the type of analysis you will have to carry out. Therefore, it is important from the outset to recognise the relationship between research questions and research methods. The different types of research questions that you can consider are outlined in Table 2.1, with an example question for each. Understanding what type of question you are asking will make the process of designing a suitable methodology more straightforward.

From Research Questions to Research Methods

When designing your research question, it is important that you always consider **how** you would go about answering it before finalising your

Table 2.1 Types of Research Questions

Types of question	Explanation	Example
Descriptive questions	These are "what" questions. These questions don't try to explain a phenomenon	What percentage of UK homeowners have been victims of burglary in the last 12 months?
Comparative questions	These questions compare one set of occurrences with another	Are older women more fearful of crime than younger women?
Correlational questions	These questions look for effects or influences of one variable on another	Do previous experiences with the police affect people's perception of them?
Interpretive questions	These questions try to make interpretations about people's perceptions and/or experiences	What do people perceive to be the most important factors to reduce crime in their area?
Exploratory questions	These questions are intended to explore a particular topic without attaching preconceived ideas	What do students do to ensure their safety when partaking in the night-time economy?
Evaluative questions	These questions try to evaluate the usefulness in the application of ideas and/or practices	How useful is the theory of rational choice in explaining acts of terrorism?

question. It is common that research questions need to be reworded or adjusted if the initial wording is not achievable methodologically or ethically. Students often make the mistake of thinking that undertaking a library-based piece of work means that research methods are not applicable, but this is the wrong approach to take. Whether you are undertaking a library-based or empirical project, you still need to consider what approach is required to answer the research question. Chapters 5 and 6 will be discussing particular methods and sampling in more detail, but for now, let's consider methodological considerations for the different types of questions.

The first consideration is **ethics**. You ought to ensure that what you are asking can be answered in a way that meets your institution's ethical procedure. It is possible to ask questions about sensitive topics and vulnerable groups, but you may not be able to collect your own data due to ethical restrictions. If you cannot collect your own data, then it is worthwhile exploring other avenues such as secondary data analysis or undertaking a library-based dissertation.

The second consideration is whether you have (or can get) **the data** needed to answer a question. For example, if you pose a question such as "Has news reporting of Brexit changed people's views of immigration?" (from Activity 4 in Box 2.6) you would need to know what people's views were before Brexit to be able to measure whether any change had occurred. If you are looking at "before and after" effects of something, it is important to make sure you have the "before and after" data. Similarly, if you are comparing two (or more) social groups, ensure that you have access to data for both groups.

The third consideration is your **own skills in research methods**. It is likely that you will have received research methods training as part of your course; however, there may be some methods that you are more (or less) comfortable using. It would be unadvisable to devise a question that would require a method such as quantitative analysis, if you are not confident in using this method. In this scenario you should look again at your research question and alter it so that it can be answered using methods you are more comfortable with.

Quantitative research questions focus more on descriptive, comparative, and correlational questions. Quantitative research focuses on "what, when, and where" type questions. Qualitative research questions are more likely to be exploratory and interpretive, with the focus being more on understanding and discovery. There are, of course, exceptions, and it will very much depend on what your question is. For example, evaluative questions can be answered quantitatively– for example, if you were measuring the impact a new security measure had on crime rates– but they can also be answered qualitatively, to provide an in-depth understanding of the impact a measure has had. Therefore, it is important to have a very clear research question with a purpose when you design it. You can read more on the suitability of research methods for types of questions by looking at Bryman (2016) and Walliman (2006). Have a go at the activity in Box 2.8 to start becoming familiar with different types of research questions.

Box 2.8   Student Activity 5

Activity 5: Identifying Methods for Questions

Can you think of the most suitable research method for the following research questions? Consider what type of question it is and what type of data you would need to collect to answer it:

- What percentage of UK homeowners have been victims of burglary in the last 12 months?
- Are older women more fearful of crime than younger women?
- Do previous experiences with the police affect people's perception of them?
- What do people perceive to be the most important factors to reduce crime in their area?
- What do students do to ensure their safety when partaking in the night-time economy?
- How useful is the theory of rational choice in explaining acts of terrorism?

Summary and Checklist

This chapter has outlined the process of narrowing down your topic and devising a suitable research question. You should now be more confident in undertaking this process by following the steps and guidance provided. Before moving on to the next chapter make sure you have completed the checklist in Box 2.9.

Box 2.9   Checklist

1   Identified the reading required to narrow down your topic ☐
2   Brainstormed possible research questions ☐
3   Ensured your question meets the criteria set out ☐
4   Identified the most suitable methodological approach to answer your question ☐
5   Completed Activities 3, 4 and 5 ☐

Further Reading

Bryman, A. (2016) *Social Research Methods*. 5th edn. Oxford: Oxford University Press. Chapter 4.

Rudestam, K.E. and Newton, R.R. (2015) *Surviving Your Dissertation: A Comprehensive Guide To Content And Process*. London: Sage. Chapter 2.

Walliman, N. (2006) *Social Research Methods*. London: Sage. Chapter 4.

Chapter 3

Access and Ethical Issues in Criminology Dissertations

Overview

One of the major obstacles for undertaking undergraduate dissertations is the ethical issues that need to be addressed. These issues are not wholly unique to criminology; however, the very nature of criminology, which focuses on vulnerable people, closed institutions, and illegal activity, means that ethics can be a barrier to some types of research students would like to undertake. This chapter outlines key access and ethical challenges that are specifically related to criminological research, explains why they are problematic, and offers suggestions of alternative types of research.

By the end of this chapter you should:

- Understand the importance of ethics when undertaking a dissertation
- Understand the ethical obligations of researchers
- Appreciate the access difficulties for criminological research
- Be familiar with the key ethical issues in undertaking a dissertation
- Be able to make assessments of ethical risks in research

Ethical Obligations

The term "ethics" is something you will have heard a lot during your time studying research methods, and you should be familiar with what ethics in research refers to. Ethics are often viewed as a procedural requirement, whereby students complete a form and get approval from an ethics committee. In fact, ethics in criminological research are much more than just the procedural requirements of getting committee approval, so before we discuss particular ethical issues, it is

DOI: 10.4324/9781003016335-4

important to consider the importance of your ethical obligation when undertaking research.

When you undertake research for a dissertation, you are fundamentally trying to find something out, answer a question, and contribute to academic knowledge. However, in this endeavour all researchers should act with honesty and integrity. All student research projects need to consider their responsibility towards the discipline of criminology, towards any research participants, and towards their institution (see Wahidin and Moore, 2011). Ethical considerations must be undertaken at every stage of the research process: the design, data collection, data analysis, writing up, and dissemination. Being an ethical researcher is about more than just completing an ethics application form; it means ensuring that your actions throughout the research process are ethical, and this can include ethical issues that arise which were not anticipated. Guillemin and Gillam (2004) distinguish ethics as *procedural ethics* and *ethics in practice*. **Procedural ethics** are the stages of formal approval, normally involving the completion of a form stating what the ethical issues are and how you intend to address them. This procedure normally takes place at the start of a research project, and empirical work should not continue until this has been approved. This will usually take the form of an internal application that you make to your school or faculty. **Ethics in practice**, on the other hand, are the ethical issues that arise during the research process once you have commenced your data collection. Often these are unanticipated ethical issues that you must deal with, and they may even pose a moral or legal dilemma. Box 3.1 lists some potential unforeseen ethical issues that can occur during empirical research projects. Take some time to consider how you would deal with such issues and whether any of these could have been prevented.

When you undertake your own research, it is essential that you consider carefully what the possible consequences of your project may be. It is not always possible to predict all ethical issues that may arise during your project; however, in the early stages of a dissertation you need to take time to consider all the potential issues to minimise any negative consequences.

It is important that you fully understand your ethical obligations throughout the research process by discussing these with your supervisor and referring to the suggested further reading at the end of this chapter. If you are undertaking research involving documents, it is also essential that you ensure you have permission to use those documents for your project.

Box 3.1 Potential Unforeseen Ethical Issues

Examples of potential unforeseen ethical issues:

- An interviewee breaks down in tears during an interview after one of the questions triggers a memory of an unpleasant experience
- A survey participant states they intend to commit a crime
- A focus group participant discloses they have committed a crime and have gone undetected
- An interviewee discloses they have been a victim of a sexual assault
- A police officer discloses malpractice
- A participant requests to be named in the write-up
- A participant does not think the write-up of the findings is an accurate representation of what they said

Codes of Ethics

Codes of ethics are ethical principles published by governing bodies or institutions. Your own university will have a code of ethics, which will clearly state what researchers ought to do to ensure their research is ethical. The British Society of Criminology (BSC) has its own statement of ethics, specifically designed for people undertaking research on crime and criminal justice. In the BSC Statement it is made clear that researchers have an ethical obligation to their institution, their research participants, their colleagues, themselves, and the discipline of criminology.

The key principles of ethical research are: ensuring you **avoid any harm** to participants, which could be physical, psychological, or emotional; **minimising your own risk** by ensuring you keep yourself safe throughout the research process; **avoiding deception**, making sure you explain fully the purpose of the research and what is expected from participants; and abiding by the UK **General Data Protection Regulation** (UK GDPR), ensuring that you store and destroy any data securely. All research with human participants should, as a minimum, provide participants with an information sheet explaining the research project, what their participation will involve, how their data will be used, and contact details of the researcher and supervisor. Participants should also be provided with a consent form that details what they are consenting to by participating. This goes towards ensuring you are obtaining **informed consent** and that participants are taking part in your study voluntarily. **Confidentiality and anonymity** are also important in any empirical research with human participants. It is not always straightforward to guarantee confidentiality to participants, because in some cases you have to break confidentiality for safety or legal reasons. For example, in my own research with police officers, I guaranteed confidentiality unless they disclosed information that would put themselves or somebody else in immediate danger. It is important that you consider in the early stages under what circumstances and on what grounds you would not keep information confidential, and you must ensure this is communicated clearly to your participants. For further guidance on ethical principles and measures you can use to uphold them, please see Caulfield and Hill (2018) in the suggested further reading.

Understanding the codes of ethics for your own institutions and the processes involved to ensure you are undertaking ethical projects is something you should do at the very start of the dissertation process. If your initial project idea would pose problematic ethical issues, then you may need to adjust your focus or your sample to avoid complications. It is best to anticipate these early on rather than trying to address them later in the research process. To help you understand some key ethical problems that can arise, the remainder of this chapter will discuss some example ethical issues that can arise in criminology dissertation projects.

Accessing Criminal Justice Institutions

Table 1.1 in Chapter 1 outlined the complexities of undertaking research with different criminal justice institutions, and several of these complexities relate to access issues. Many criminal justice institutions are regarded as closed institutions, meaning they are not open to the general public to observe. This includes, but is not limited to: family courts, youth offender institutions, prisons, police stations, and rehabilitation centres. Accessing such institutions is limited because it is the duty of those institutions to protect people legally and morally. It is important that individuals within these institutions (whether they be victims, suspects, witnesses, or employees) are not exposed to potential harms that can be caused by research.

Criminal justice institutions, such as prisons and police forces, have their own application systems for people wanting to undertake research. These research application processes can take months, and there is no guarantee that you will be granted access. Any application would need to demonstrate the benefit of the research to the institution and provide a strong justification for why the research is necessary. Obstacles can be created for researchers accessing criminal justice organisations because these institutions do not want to be subjected to scrutiny (see Duke, 2002) and a student's position as an "outsider" (see Brown, 1996) can make this an even greater challenge. Undertaking research with individuals who work in these institutions has its own ethical issues, particularly power relations, that need to be considered. Negotiating with gatekeepers to the research sites can be a lengthy process, and these gatekeepers can grant or deny access to certain spaces and people in the research process. This can ultimately impact on your research, because you may not have complete control over who you get to recruit to your study and the gatekeepers may request that you share data with them. Identifying who the potential gatekeepers are and the impact or influence they can have on your study is vitally important. Have a look at the activity in Box 3.2 to get you thinking about some of the potential problems with researching criminal justice institutions.

Having existing contacts with people in criminal justice organisations is not a guarantee that you can gain access. Caution should be taken not to assume that your prior connection to a criminal justice organisation will enable you to research it or the people it works with. In each of the examples in Box 3.2, the students have made such assumptions without consideration of the role of the gatekeepers, the personal relationship conflicts, or the dangers they could be putting themselves and their participants in. That is not to say it is impossible to research closed institutions, and some undergraduate dissertations are successful in doing this (see Taylor, 2019). However, careful consideration needs to be put into the planning to ensure access can be granted and that it would not impact on the integrity of the research project. The time-consuming and procedural access requirements are one barrier to undertaking research with criminal justice organisations, but the subject area and the sample population are other reasons why this can be an obstacle.

Box 3.2 Student Activity 6

Activity 6: Researching Criminal Justice Institutions

For each of the examples below, note down the following:

- What are the potential access and ethical issues?
- Who could be potentially harmed or deceived?
- Would it be a suitable project for an undergraduate dissertation? Why/why not?

1 Researching police discretion

Jack is planning to undertake an observation of police officers patrolling Manchester on Friday and Saturday nights. Jack's mother is a police officer who has said Jack can go out with her and observe how they police the night-time economy. Jack deems this to be a great opportunity as he already has access and knows his mother will look after him.

2 Researching rehabilitation

Sam's dissertation is exploring effective methods of rehabilitation for women leaving prison. Sam has been volunteering at a local women's rehabilitation centre and wants to use her contacts there to interview some of the women about what programmes they have found to be most effective. The centre manager has agreed to the project on the condition that they get to approve all interview questions first and that a centre employee is present for all the interviews.

3 Researching prison security

Jessica is proposing to undertake observational research to explore the security measures for visitors to different prison establishments. Jessica is currently employed by the prison service and therefore already has security clearance for going into prisons. Jessica knows the prison governors and some members of prison staff, so does not deem herself to be an outsider.

Vulnerability and Sensitive Topics

Students are often interested in researching topics with people who could be considered vulnerable; this could include children, people with addictions, and people with poor mental health. Individuals are considered vulnerable if there are limitations in their ability to give informed consent; this may be due to personal characteristics, such as age or disability, or situational circumstances, such as being coerced or being under the influence of drugs and/or alcohol. Many topics in criminology cover vulnerable populations and therefore it is understandable that many students would like to research these topics for a final-year project. However, safeguarding participants from harm is a core ethical principle and, in many cases, student dissertation proposals are rejected because of the vulnerability of the participant sample. If your research project does not intend to sample persons considered vulnerable, you should also ensure during the research process that vulnerability does not become a factor. For instance, if you are undertaking interviews, you should be confident that the participants are not under the influence of any drugs or alcohol that could impact on their ability to provide informed consent.

Researching sensitive topics is another area where ethical considerations have to be prioritised. Renzetti and Lee (1993: ix) define sensitive topics as those that are *intimate, discreditable or incriminating* – which, in criminology, can apply to a whole range of different topics such as victimisation, addiction, or offending. Sensitive topics are those that have the potential to cause harm, embarrassment, or distress to either participants or researchers, or both. Wincup (2017) argues that often the term is used when researching vulnerable groups (such as children), but it can also apply to people in positions of power (see Lee, 1993). When designing your research study, such as survey or interview topics, you should put yourself in the position of the participant and consider whether the topic could be deemed as sensitive. Asking people about topics that could trigger painful memories, asking them to report on traumatic events, or getting them to discuss embarrassing situations should be avoided. It can often be difficult to predict the sensitivity of a research topic, but you can mitigate issues by scrutinising your topic and research questions from the participants' point of view. Look at the activity in Box 3.3; can you think of how this problem could have been prevented or how Jun can resolve this ethical issue?

There are measures you can take in research to ensure that potentially sensitive issues are addressed before, during, and after field work takes place (see Deakin, 2011). Including trigger warnings on your participant information sheets and consent forms allows participants to make a fully informed decision before taking part. Including details of support services in research materials (such as surveys, information sheets, or any follow-up correspondence) to direct participants to services should they require additional support ensures that you have considered the welfare of your participants. If undertaking surveys, you can also make potentially sensitive questions optional so that participants do not have to answer them. If you are undertaking interviews or focus groups, you can ask participants whether there is anything they would not be comfortable discussing, and use body language cues to pick up whether your participants appear to be in any kind of discomfort.

Box 3.3   Student Activity 7

Activity 7: Researching Student Burglaries

Jun is undertaking a survey of students' measures to prevent burglary in their privately rented accommodation. Jun has provided an information sheet advising participants that their responses will remain anonymous and that no personal details will be collected. Jun does not deem burglary to be a sensitive topic, and the survey is only asking participants about the measures they take to secure their property and belongings. Jun does not collect any identifiable data, to ensure that the survey is completely anonymous. Unbeknown to Jun, one of the participants becomes upset while completing the survey due to being a victim of burglary. The survey made them question whether the burglary was their fault because they had not taken preventative measures. This causes the participant distress and it brings back memories of the burglary.

Questions to consider:

1. What could Jun have done prior to commencing fieldwork?
2. What could Jun have done during the fieldwork to support participants who might have felt this way?

Assessing Risk in Research

It is very unlikely that you would intentionally put yourself in a dangerous situation to carry out your dissertation; however, some dissertation topics can lead to you putting yourself at risk, and these need to be mitigated against from the outset. If we take Example 1 from Box 3.2, Jack may find himself in a dangerous position if the police must deal with a potentially violent encounter; this could cause Jack distress or put him in physical danger. It is ultimately up to you as the researcher not to put yourself in potentially dangerous situations, and you should not rely on others to guarantee your safety. Many universities now ask students to complete a risk assessment prior to commencing any fieldwork, and this is to ensure your safety. Safeguarding yourself during the research is vital, and this is something that should not be overlooked in the planning stages. Considerations must be made in terms of where research is conducted, how you will travel safely to and from research sites, how you will ensure your emotional wellbeing is protected, and how you will protect yourself from any potential physical danger.

Some students may also want to undertake a particular piece of research because of personal reasons; for example, because they have been a victim of a crime, or have had personal experiences going through the criminal justice system, or have family or friends who have been directly affected by crime. In these circumstances it is always important to protect your **own wellbeing** and to avoid topics that may cause you upset or distress. Therefore, it is important in your research design to have a strong rationale for your proposal, so that even if the topic has a personal connection to you, the dissertation serves a purpose. If the topic itself is going to be distressing for you to read and write about, then it is recommended that you choose a topic you are more detached from. I suggest you **speak to your supervisor** if you have chosen a topic due to personal experience, to ensure that your supervisor is confident you will not come to any harm.

Devising Alternative Research Projects

It is often the case that access and ethical issues will prevent you from undertaking your chosen research project, but that does not prevent you from researching a topic using alternative methods. In Table 3.1 are examples of initial research ideas that have been ethically problematic, with examples of alternative methods. If your chosen topic does not meet the code of ethics or you cannot get access, then I recommend

Table 3.1 Alternative Project Suggestions

Initial Research Project	Ethical Issues	Alternative Project
Survey urban and rural residents about what crime they have been a victim of in the last two years	Potentially distressing to ask people about victimisation	Undertake secondary data analysis of the Crime Survey for England and Wales
Interview criminal gang members about the social issues in their communities	Potentially dangerous situation for the student to be researching people they know are involved in illegal activity	Interview employees/volunteers of community groups who are helping people leave criminal gangs
Surveying prisoners about what prison programmes they use to help improve their mental health	Difficulties accessing prison establishments Prisoners with mental health illnesses are a vulnerable population	Undertake a library-based dissertation that critically examines previous research on programmes designed to improve mental health in prison
Interviewing witnesses about their experiences of giving evidence in trials	Accessing witnesses could be ethically challenging due to anonymity and confidentiality Asking people to recall witnessing crime could also be very distressing	Undertake research with Witness Support services to understand what they believe are the core challenges for witness services

you devise alternative strategies that still allow you to research your preferred topic. This may require you to adjust your research question slightly, but it should still enable you to research a topic of interest.

Summary and Checklist

This chapter has discussed some of the key access and ethical issues that may arise if you choose to undertake empirical research. If your project has any potential to cause yourself or your participants any harm or distress, then I recommend you consider revising your topic or your methods to minimise ethical problems. Use the checklist in

Box 3.4 to help you with ethical considerations when designing your project.

Box 3.4 Checklist

1   Read the ethical review procedures for your school/
    department   ☐
2. Note down any potential access or ethical issues with
    your topic   ☐
3   Discuss any potential ethical issues with your
    supervisor   ☐
4   Read around ethical guidelines for your chosen
    project/topic   ☐
5   Ensure your research design abides by the British
    Society of Criminology's code of ethics   ☐
6   Devise an alternative project that still enables you to
    research your chosen topic   ☐
7   Complete activities 6 and 7 of this chapter   ☐

Further Reading

British Society of Criminology (BSC) (2015). *Statement of Ethics.* Available at: www.britsoccrim.org/ethics/ [Accessed 9 December 2021].

Caufield, L. and Hill, J. (2018) *Criminological Skills and research for Beginners 2nd Edition.* London: Routledge. Chapter 7.

Wahidin, A. and Moore, L. (2011) 'Ethics and Criminological Research', in Davies, P., Francis, P. and Jupp, V. (Eds) *Doing Criminological Research 2nd Edition.* London: Sage, pp. 287–307.

Chapter 4

Literature Reviews

Overview

All undergraduate dissertations should contain a literature review, no matter what approach you are using. They can be one aspect of a dissertation that students struggle with, arguably because there is often uncertainty about what a literature review is, why it is important, and how it should be written. This chapter will demonstrate the importance of literature reviews for ensuring well-formulated research questions and methodologies. It will move to explain how to write an effective literature review and how a literature review differs from other pieces of writing, and will give tips for structuring the review. The chapter will discuss searching for literature by providing suggestions for useful resources where literature and policy can be sourced.

By the end of this chapter you should know:

- The purpose of a literature review
- How to identify relevant sources
- How to write a literature review
- How to structure a literature review

What Is a Literature Review?

A literature review is a critical evaluation of previous literature centring around a particular topic. The role of the literature review is to discuss what we already know on a topic, both theoretically and empirically, and utilise it as a justification for undertaking your own research. Reviewing previous literature will help you to determine what research has already been undertaken on a topic and to identify

DOI: 10.4324/9781003016335-5

the applicable theoretical frameworks, what gaps exist in the literature, and emerging areas of importance. Literature can consist of a range of sources, including books, journal articles, policy reports, research briefings, conference proceedings, online content, and theses. A literature review **showcases your in-depth knowledge** of a topic, demonstrating you understand the main arguments in the field, know who the key authors are, and have a good grasp of what research is lacking. If a detailed literature review is not provided, then you run the risk of developing arguments and conclusions that have already been covered by previous authors, which in turn would show gaps in your knowledge. Box 4.1 lists the key purposes of the literature review.

Box 4.1 Top Tips for Literature Reviews

Top Tips: What a Literature Review Should Demonstrate

- What existing research and theory already exists in relation to your topic
- Your knowledge and understanding of the literature, including the core theories, debates, research methods and findings
- What gaps in knowledge exist for your chosen topic; this could be in relation to theoretical gaps, gaps in content, or methodological gaps
- How your research fits within the existing body of literature, and what it will add or contribute to the academic debates.

The Distinctiveness of Literature Reviews

Before moving on to discuss how to undertake a literature review, let us begin by differentiating literature reviews from other forms of writing. This should help you to understand the distinctiveness of a literature review from other types of assessments you may have undertaken at university.

Devising and writing a literature review is different from writing an academic essay. In an essay, you start off with a question (usually), and your objective is to find sources to support your arguments that will answer the question. In a literature review, you start off with a topic and synthesise the sources so that the literature is the focus of discussion, and you generate a research question not already addressed in previous research. Therefore, it is important to undertake a review of literature in the early stages before settling on a research question. Your research question should be guided by what literature and research does or does not already exist. Students who devise a research question before reviewing any literature tend to face difficulties in demonstrating that their project is new or innovative in the field; this is because some research questions chosen by students have already been answered in existing works. The tip here is not to approach the literature review like you would an essay; rather, **start with the literature** and allow your research focus to grow from there. A literature review also differs from an essay in that it brings the sources together in a critical manner by discussing different findings, theoretical approaches, and methodologies. The aim is to demonstrate you understand *the works* of authors in the field – not just what authors have argued but how they have come to those arguments, and what evidence and/or theoretical frameworks underpin the claims they are making.

Another common error that supervisors see in literature reviews is mistaking them for annotated bibliographies. An annotated bibliography describes and evaluates sources individually, in alphabetical order; the aim of an annotated bibliography is to produce a well-organised list of sources with concise descriptions and explanations. In a literature review, sources are combined – synthesised – to evaluate core debates and findings and critically discuss multiple sources to determine where disagreements may lie.

The remainder of this chapter will take you through the different steps of a literature review, from devising keyword searches to structuring the literature review chapter. Figure 4.1 provides an illustration

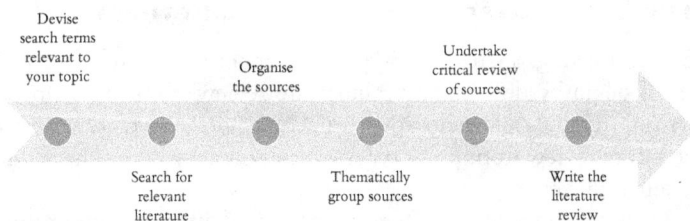

Figure 4.1 The Literature Review Process.

of the process of producing a literature review, and we will start with how to identify relevant sources.

Identifying Relevant Sources

Knowing where to start with a literature review can often be the most difficult stage, particularly if you have a broad topic for your dissertation. This section offers guidance on searching for relevant literature and knowing what literature should or should not be included.

Devising Your Search Terms

It is likely that you undertook some initial reading to choose the topic for your dissertation. Once you have your chosen topic, it is time to read widely to identify what work is relevant to your project. To help you start, try the four steps outlined in Box 4.2.

Box 4.2 Student Activity 8

Activity 8: Planning Your Literature Search

Step 1: Note down key words associated with your topic; you can use these later to help you search for relevant sources

Step 2: Note down key authors; look at textbooks and edited collections to establish who are notable authors on your topic

Step 3: Note down the types of sources you need. For instance, if your topic is policy focused, what sort of policy documents will you need to source? If your topic is more legal focused, what legislation or case laws do you need to locate?

Step 4: Note down any specific criteria you have in your topic; for example, you might want your literature limited to a certain time period, or location, or discipline

---

Identifying keywords is an important process for any literature review because you will need to use these for whatever search platform you choose. Using your topic, try brainstorming or mapping (see Smith et al., 2009) words related to your topics and consider what synonyms can be used for keywords identified. Figure 4.2 is an example of how a keyword such as "young people" can be explored with different

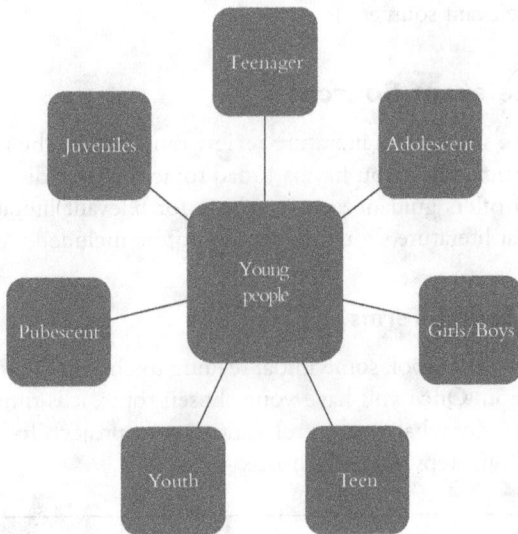

Figure 4.2 Keyword Brainstorming.

terminology, and these alternative words can be added to your bank of keywords for searching.

Once you have built up a catalogue of terms, you can start to narrow down your search terms by identifying what specific keywords go together, and terms you want to avoid; for example, if your dissertation is looking at the police responses to burglary in rural areas, choose the main keywords for your search:

Policing AND Burglary AND Rural

Similarly, you can create search sentences for terms you are not interested in to help filter out unwanted pieces of literature; for example, if a student was interested in police responses to violence but did not want literature on domestic violence, they could use the search:

Policing AND Violence NOT Domestic

Chapter 2 outlined the importance of having a clear and narrow focus for your dissertation, and this is certainly the case for devising your literature review. The broader your topic is, the more difficult it is to undertake concise literature searches. Being overwhelmed with what literature to look for is often a consequence of not having a clear focus from the outset. If you are finding it difficult to identify keywords, it may be that you need to narrow down your topic.

Identifying key authors is also an important aspect for literature reviews, because a literature review should demonstrate your knowledge and understanding of leading work in the field. It is likely that you have chosen a topic based on some prior learning and therefore should have an idea of some key authors in advance. However, if you have chosen an entirely new topic, you will need to identify leading authors by looking at who is routinely publishing work in that field – textbooks, monographs, and journal articles – and who is routinely cited by other authors.

Finally, starting to develop a search plan can really help with your literature review. Consider whether there are specific types of literature you need to source, such as legislation, policy documents, or official reports. Again, look at your research topic and decide what sort of criteria you need to place on your searches; for instance:

•   Are you only interested in work published within a certain time period?
•   Do you need to include work based on international research?
•   Are there particular socio-demographics that apply to your topic?

Being very clear at the beginning can really help you undertake a focused search for literature and ensure you do not spend unnecessary time searching for irrelevant literature. It is worthwhile taking time on this part of the dissertation as it will build a strong foundation for the remaining work.

Search Strategies

Once you have gone through the four steps in Box 4.2 and started to create search sentences, it is time to start searching for relevant literature. There are different ways you can search for literature, and it is likely you will combine a range of these when compiling your literature review.

Figure 4.3 lists the search process most students will undertake. The first place to look is your university library catalogue. This will enable you to enter your search terms, and many catalogues will offer the opportunity to narrow down your search by type of source, subject area, and date range. Google Scholar is another useful search engine;

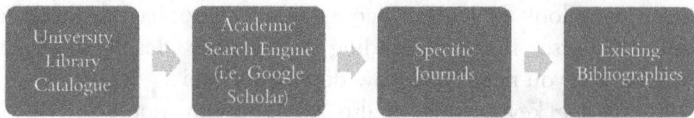

Figure 4.3 Searching for Literature.

again, using your keywords or core authors, you can search for books, chapters and journal articles that might be relevant to your topic. The benefit of Google Scholar is that under each entry there is a link to click to see what other sources have cited the source, which is a great way to snowball sample your reading and find relevant pieces of literature. You can also search for useful literature within sources you have read by utilising their reference lists or bibliographies. Using bibliographies in existing work can help you create a list of potential sources that might be relevant to your project.

When using a database such as your university library catalogue, journal databases, or Google Scholar, you must be flexible with your keywords; sometimes the keyword is too narrow to return useful search results, which is why noting down related words can be helpful. Jensen and Laurie (2016: 35) offer a nice example of this and showcase how just altering the keywords slightly can ensure you get better results in your searches.

Once you begin searching, you may become overwhelmed by the amount of different literature available; however, many of your search results may not to be relevant to your project. When searching books, you will want to read the title, the **synopsis** and possibly the introductory chapter to be sure the book is relevant. For journal articles you should read the title and the **abstract**, which will give you an indication of whether the article is worth adding to your list of readings. Research and policy reports will usually contain an **executive summary** at the beginning, which will provide you with an overview of the source's contents. Utilising these strategies to determine whether a source is relevant without having to read the whole book/article/report will ensure you are using your time effectively during this stage. Using the advanced search features of online databases to narrow down results is another method for reducing the feeling of being overwhelmed.

Keep a document listing all the sources you have identified as relevant, noting the full bibliographic reference and any links needed to access it. This can be helpful for several reasons:

- It helps you keep track of what literature you have found on what topics
- You can check off sources after you have read them
- It ensures you do not forget where you accessed the source in the first place
- You can group sources together according to themes or criteria to help structure your reading
- You save yourself time at the end trying to find sources for when you need to write your bibliography

Effective Reading

Once you have collected sources relevant to your topic, it is time to undertake your reading. This is the most time-consuming stage of a literature review– but also the most important, so it should not be rushed. If you are undecided what readings to start with, Burnett (2009) suggests starting with the classic texts for your topic to provide a foundation for everything else you read.

When you undertake your reading, you will want to ensure you take effective notes and keep your notes organised. Everyone has different techniques for note-taking, and you will know the method that works best for you. One suggestion is to have a template for note-taking which ensures that when you are reading, you are noting down the same key information for everything you read. An example template has been provided in Table 4.1, but you could create your own, adding in more columns such as key concepts, discipline, location of research, and so on. The suggestion is that you have an organised system for note-taking that will make the process of grouping multiple sources together much easier. You could also use it to note useful quotes or relevant figures/diagrams (not forgetting to include the page number).

The most important aspect of the note-taking is your overall impression of what you have read and applying your critical thinking to it. You want to be asking yourself the following and taking clear detailed notes on your answers:

- What are the overarching arguments of this source?
- Why is the author making those arguments?
- What are they basing their arguments on?
- How does it compare to other sources on this topic?

Table 4.1 Template for Organised Note-Taking

	Literature 1	Literature 2	Literature 3
Full bibliographical reference			
Type of source			
Aim of the source			
Theoretical approach			
Type of research			
Methodology			
Key findings/conclusions			
Strengths of source			
Limitations of source			
Overall impression			

When reviewing the literature, you should not simply note down what an author has said but use the questions above to evaluate the source. Consider what methods the author(s) applied and how valid and reliable these are, evaluate whether arguments are supported with evidence, and note if anything is lacking in the evidence or discussion. Applying this critical thinking while reading the sources will make it easier when it comes to writing your literature review, because you will have already reviewed the information in a critical way.

Another important thing to remember when undertaking your reading is to ensure that you are always linking it to **your project**:

- Where does the source fit in to your dissertation?
- Why is it relevant?
- How will it be useful to your dissertation?
- What can you learn from it?

If a source does not seem relevant after reading it the first time, it may be that you will return to it later in the research process, so always keep the notes of what you have read.

While undertaking your reading, you should make links between the different sources you are drawing on. Consider whether similar studies have similar conclusions. If there are differences, note down why this might be; it may be the methodological approach, the sample, or the theoretical frameworks they are using that leads them to draw different conclusions. Utilising a note-keeping system, such as the template provided in Table 4.1, enables you to compare your readings in one place, and you can make notes of where similarities and differences lie. You may want to add some of the prompt questions discussed here to columns in your note-taking template to ensure that you are consistently engaging in a critical review.

Once you have completed your reading, you can begin to group sources of literature together under different themes. How you decide upon those themes will very much depend on the focus of your topic and how you want to present themes. You may want to group readings together according to their theoretical frameworks, type of study, timeframe, key topics, findings and conclusions, or type of publication. It is often at this stage that you start to identify what further reading you need to undertake. If there are key themes coming through from your literature or areas you need to read up on more widely, then start the process again.

Writing the Literature Review

Once you have completed your reading, it is time to start writing the literature review. You should start by devising an organised structure for your literature review that is clear to follow for whoever reads it. The following section will offer some guidance on ensuring a coherent structure and how you should write the literature review.

Introduce the Literature Review

All literature review chapters should start with an introduction of one or two paragraphs. The introduction should state clearly how the literature review is laid out, what the aim of the literature review is, and how the literature review relates to your project. This does not need to be in great depth or discussion, but rather should enable the reader to establish the relevance of the literature you have chosen to review.

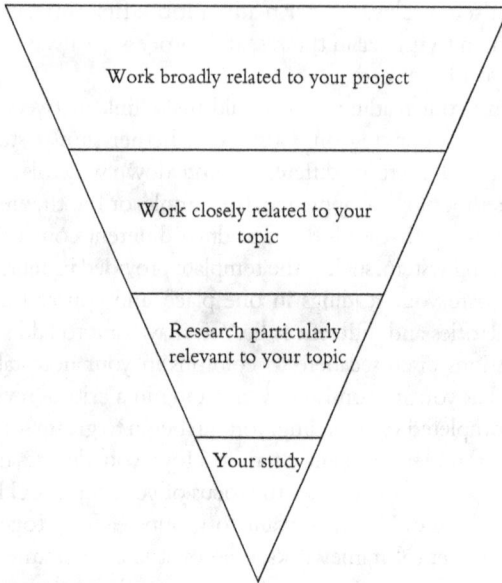

Figure 4.4 The Funnel Method.

The Main Body of the Literature Review

There is no right or wrong way to structure the main body of a literature review, but it does require a coherent structure. One method of structuring your literature review is the funnel method (see Figure 4.4). Using this method, you start the main body of the literature review by discussing the broadest literature related to your topic; this could be the underpinning theoretical framework, it could be the classic works in the field, or it could be a critical discussion of the topic in the broadest sense. From there, you move on to discussing work closely related to your topic, looking at the general key issues from the literature. You then move on to critically discuss work directly related to your study before finishing the literature review with how it all provides a basis and justification for your study. A worked example of the funnel method has been provided in Box 4.3, where you should see how the literature starts with the broader work on the key topics before gradually moving through to the more specific work. This approach enables you to frame the literature you are using within the wider academic field and provides your reader with the wider context to the subject area.

The structure will very much depend on your topic. For instance, if you are undertaking a historical dissertation, it may make more sense to

structure the main body according to key periods of time. If your dissertation is going to have a policy focus, then it may be beneficial to critically discuss the academic literature in one section and the policy literature
in a different section. Structuring the literature in the most appropriate
way will take time and may involve drafting several alternative structures
until you find the one that will work best for your project.

Box 4.3 Worked Example of the Funnel Method

This example is taken from a published undergraduate dissertation by Debo-Aina (2021). The dissertation explored *How the
Media and Political (Mis)Representations of UK Drill Music Affects
the Lives and Identities of Black Youth in South London.*

She used the funnel method approach by starting the literature review with the bigger issues facing black culture in
the UK; she then moved on to discuss the literature on the
media's role in portraying black culture as dangerous. The literature review moves on to offer an insight into more specifics
of drill music and the research undertaken on how it is policed
in the UK. The literature review ends by clearly stating the
gaps in existing research and how her dissertation will address
those gaps.

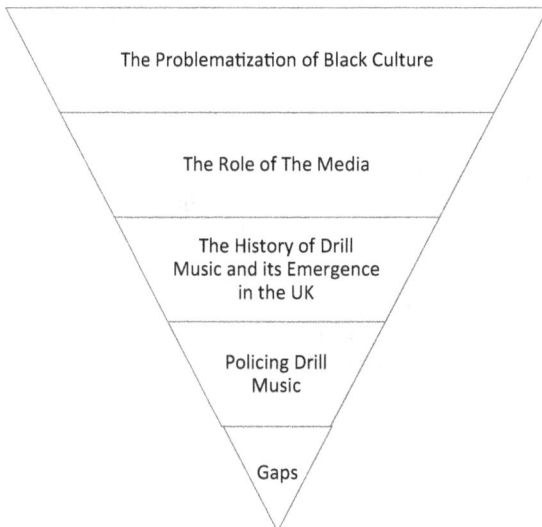

The Problematization of Black Culture

The Role of The Media

The History of Drill
Music and its Emergence
in the UK

Policing Drill
Music

Gaps

When it comes to the actual writing of the literature review, you need to ensure that your style of writing meets academic standards. A literature review should not:

- Be a description of what we already know
- Be a list of different authors/studies
- Be based around only a handful of sources

When writing the literature review, you want to make certain you are demonstrating your critical thinking skills, which in turn will help demonstrate your knowledge and understanding of key work in the field. If you are making core arguments in your literature review, be sure to have more than one piece of evidence to substantiate your claims. To make your arguments persuasive in the literature review, you ought to synthesise a range of evidence that will ensure your claims are convincing. You should raise questions over any methodological or theoretical limitations in previous research, while also highlighting strengths of previous research. While the literature review is predominantly addressing the perspective of others, it is important that the reader gets a sense of **your position** and what your views of the existing literature are. Making sure you include your own commentary on the literature – its strengths and limitations – will help to strengthen your justifications for your own project.

Concluding Your Literature Review

All literature reviews should include a conclusion that will determine what the outcome of the literature review was and how it feeds into the development of your research project. A conclusion should discuss what the overarching message of the literature review is, what we already know, what the gaps are in the existing literature, and how your project will contribute to existing knowledge. Box 4.4 provides two nice examples of partial conclusions of literature reviews. You should notice they discuss the current existing literature on the topic while drawing the reader's attention to the gaps. Both nicely frame their own research project by demonstrating what contribution their research will make to the topics. The conclusion should also signpost to the reader what will be coming next in your dissertation – what will follow on from your review of the literature.

Box 4.4 Examples of Literature Review Conclusions

Example 1: Jacklin (2020: 32)

In conclusion, the current research on green groups covers a range of issues, including interactions with the government, with law enforcement and the public. This literature is in depth and rich, especially when examining different organisations and their history. However, in the case of analysis on Extinction Rebellion specifically there is a gap. There are virtually no studies using qualitative data or interaction with members to inform their analysis. Most of the literature is theoretical, and does not cover reasons why individuals seek to be arrested for the XR cause, or as to the effects this may have on their lives. Instead, there is a focus on how the population view them, and how they interact with the police. Beyond this, there is a lack of credible research on the topic. From the gaps identified in the literature above, this research piece has formed three research questions. These have been created for the purpose of informing what methodology should be utilised to fill these research gaps.

Example 2: Deo-Aina (2021:145)

Current research on drill music fails to explore what it means for the black community from the perspective of those who participate in the drill subculture and who might invariably be affected when it is represented as problematic. The criminalisation of drill music remains largely under-researched, especially from the perspective of those within the subculture, consequently the empirical research, which does exist, often assumes that these representations affect the black community and the ways in which they affect them. It is crucial to understand from the perspective of those who are members of the black community, especially members of the drill subculture, how and if these representations affect their personal lives and communities. Understanding the importance of drill music and its subculture to the community which disproportionately consumes and produces it will highlight the severity of these representations and censures.

Common Literature Review Questions

The literature review is one aspect of the dissertation process that supervisors get asked a lot of questions about, so it is useful to consider common questions, some of which you may be asking yourself having now read this chapter. Some of these are listed in Box 4.5.

Box 4.5 Literature Review Frequently Asked Questions

1 If I am doing a library-based dissertation, do I need a literature review?

The answer is **yes**. All dissertations need to showcase knowledge of the existing literature and pinpoint how the library-based project will contribute to existing knowledge. It is also a useful exercise to ensure your research project has not already been undertaken by someone else.

2 Can sub-headings be used in literature reviews?

The answer is **yes**. Sub-headings are a great way to signpost your reader to specific sections of your literature review. They can also be helpful for creating a coherent structure.

3 I am not sure if all the literature I have included will still be relevant after I complete the rest of the dissertation.

After you complete the first draft of your literature review, chances are you will return to it more than once to make amendments. The literature review will always be a work in progress up until you submit, and it is normal for students to rework sections, and add or take out literature during the writing-up process.

4 How long should the literature review be?

This is a common question and will very much depend on your own school/department guidance. In a 12000 word dissertation, for example, we would expect the literature review to be around 2500–3000 words. However, different lengths and different types of dissertation will have different requirements for the literature review.

5 Can I read example literature reviews?

Yes; you can access published dissertations (like the example used in this chapter) online. Your own institution may have examples for you to look at, or you can browse the collection of undergraduate dissertations on the Internet Journal of Criminology.

Summary and Checklist

This chapter has provided an overview on the role and importance of literature reviews in dissertations. All dissertations will require a review of literature to lay the foundations for the remainder of the dissertation, whether it is an empirical or conceptual project. The chapter has offered strategies for planning, undertaking, and writing your literature review, and it is recommended you undertake some of the suggested further reading at the end of the chapter which can offer additional guidance. There are several textbooks that offer in-depth guidance on reviewing literature, and it is worthwhile looking at example dissertations so you begin to understand how a literature review should be written. When you begin your literature review, use the checklist in Box 4.6 to ensure you cover all the essential components.

Box 4.6 Checklist

1 Create a literature search strategy (Activity 8)   ☐
2 Create an effective method of note-taking   ☐
3 Demonstrate a clear understanding of the topic
   and key concepts   ☐
4 Critically discuss the existing literature by comparing
   existing sources of information   ☐
5 Demonstrate a clear gap in research to justify your
   project   ☐
6 Make clear how your project will fit in with existing
   literature   ☐

Further Reading

Bryman, A. (2016) *Social Research Methods*. 5th edn. Oxford: Oxford University Press. Chapter 5.

Caufield, L. and Hill, J. (2018) *Criminological Skills and Research for Beginners.* 2nd edn. London: Routledge. Chapter 9.

Smith, K., Todd, M. and Waldman, J. (2009) *Doing Your Undergraduate Social Science Dissertation*. London: Routledge. Chapter 4.

Chapter 5

Utilising Secondary Data

Overview

The ethical limitations in criminology dissertations mean that sometimes you must rely on existing data sets to answer your research question(s). This chapter will introduce you to the benefits of existing data sets and demonstrate how they can be used to answer different types of research questions. It will provide you with examples of where data can be accessed, covering prison data, police data, court data, and victim data. This chapter will provide example dissertation topics that would benefit from the use of secondary data.

By the end of this chapter you should:

- Understand the benefits and limitations of using existing data sets
- Know where you can freely access existing crime and criminal justice statistical data
- Be able to identify different sources of pre-existing data that can be used for qualitative projects

Advantages of Using Existing Data

Chapter 3 discussed the ethical limitations of undertaking dissertations in criminology. The barriers to accessing criminal justice institutions, the inability to research people considered vulnerable, and the time and resource constraints of undergraduate projects mean that it is not always possible to collect your own data. Fortunately, there is an abundance of existing research data that you can access and analyse yourself without the ethical issues of access or the time restrictions associated with collecting the data.

DOI: 10.4324/9781003016335-6

Aside from the ethical issues, there are other benefits of using secondary data for your research. Ease of access is the first, with many data resources being publicly available and free to use. This saves you a lot of time as you don't need to collect data for yourself, which can be very time-consuming for an undergraduate project. A further benefit is that it allows you to offer something unique by generating a new insight into pre-existing data. Applying a new perspective or analysing data in a new way ensures your dissertation is unique and original even though you are using existing data. A final benefit is that it allows you to undertake longitudinal analysis over a short time frame. Much of the data available to download is collected annually, meaning you can download data covering many years to explore whether there have been any changes over time.

Limitations of Using Existing Data

All research methods come with limitations, so it is important to recognise these before you commence your research. Secondary data can be limiting if it does not meet your specific research needs; for instance, if you are exploring a particular population, social characteristic, or location that is not covered by existing data sets. Additionally, some data sets may be out of date and therefore do not offer you the opportunity to explore more contemporary issues. A further limitation is that the data collection may have been done with a particular agenda or bias that could call into question the reliability of the data. Finally, you must be careful to choose data that you can verify the quality of, as you will not have control over this. You should also check the permissions associated with documents, such as copyright restrictions, ensuring that they allow you to utilise the data for research purposes.

Accessing Statistical Data

There are a range of data sources that you can access, download, and analyse for yourself covering a range of criminal justice institutions and previous research with victims and offenders. The abundance of national and international statistics allows for a range of different topics to be researched using existing statistics. Designing and collecting quantitative data yourself can be very time-consuming, it can be costly, and often you must rely on small sample sizes. Fortunately, most statistical data on crime and criminal justice in the UK is freely available for you to access, download and analyse for yourself.

Generic resources for searching and accessing crime and justice statistics are:

- The Office for National Statistics (ONS) is a national resource that provides access to a range of publicly available data sets on crime and justice topics
- The Home Office publishes data including policing and crime prevention, the courts and sentencing, crime and victimisation, and prisons and parole in England and Wales
- The UK Data Service is one of the largest collections of data from official and independent research; it contains data from national and international research
- The Scottish Government publishes crime and victimisation data in Scotland
- The Northern Ireland Statistics and Research Agency (NISRA) can be used for crime and justice statistics in Northern Ireland
- The United Nations Office on Drugs and Crime (UNODC) produces and publishes international statistics on drugs and crime

It is worthwhile exploring these resources to see what data sets might be valuable for your research topic. The remainder of this section provides examples of some of the most useful statistical data sets that can be utilised for your dissertation. Box 5.1 and Box 5.2 provide examples of how existing data can be used in dissertations, and Table 5.1 at the end of this section provides a list of where you can access the resources discussed.

Crime and Victimisation Surveys

Crime and Victimisation surveys are annual surveys undertaken in England and Wales, Scotland and Northern Ireland. There are different surveys for each country in the UK:

- Crime Survey for England and Wales
- Scottish Crime and Victimisation Survey
- Northern Ireland Safe Community Survey

If you are interested in longitudinal data, it would be worthwhile exploring the longitudinal analysis of the Offending, Crime and Justice Survey (link in Table 5.1). You can also access international data such as the European Social Survey, the National Crime and Victimization

Survey (USA), the National Crime and Safety Survey (Australia), and the Victims of Crime Survey (South Africa), to name a few. If you are interested in crimes against businesses, it would be worthwhile exploring the Commercial Victimisation Survey (England and Wales).

These surveys can be a useful resource for downloading statistical data on crime, victimisation, perceptions of crime and perceptions of the police. The original data sets can be downloaded from the relevant websites (see Table 5.1), providing you with an abundance of data to choose from to undertake your own analysis. A further benefit is that comparative analysis can be undertaken; for example, looking at how things have changed over time, or making comparisons between countries. Box 5.1 provides examples of undergraduate dissertation topics that can utilise data sets available on the ONS website.

Box 5.1 Using Existing ONS Crime Survey Data for Dissertations

Example 1: Fear of Crime During COVID-19

Chris is interested in whether COVID-19 has an impact on people's concerns about crime. Rather than designing and distributing a survey of their own, Chris downloads the *Crime in England and Wales: Coronavirus (COVID-19) and Crime Tables* from the ONS. They undertake their own analysis to explore level of worry about crime from June to November 2020. The student also downloads the recorded crime data for the same period and compares the rates of crime with the level of worry about crime. This saves Chris time on developing and distributing a survey by utilising data that is already available.

Example 2: Victims of Child Abuse

Frankie wants to undertake empirical research on child abuse but knows that this will be difficult due to the ethical implications. Frankie is able to download the child abuse statistics from the ONS and undertakes an analysis to determine whether the nature and extent of child abuse has changed from 2016 to 2020. Utilising this data enables Frankie to undertake their own research on a sensitive topic without difficult ethical issues.

Example 3: The Dark Figure of Crime

Jessie wants to undertake a research project than explores the dark figure of crime. Jessie utilises the Crime Survey for England and Wales to compare the rates of crimes reported on the survey with the rates of crimes recorded by the police. Jessie is able to undertake their own statistical comparison of the crimes that people report on the survey and the crimes recorded by the police to understand which crimes are more or less likely to be recorded by the police.

Police Data

Gaining access to the police can be time-consuming and it can be very difficult to negotiate key gatekeepers. If you are interested in police statistics in England, Wales and Northern Ireland, you can access these at data.police.uk. This database allows you to download statistical police data, analyse it, and use it for your dissertation project. The data is official police data and includes statistics on recorded crime, arrests, stop and search, and call handling. The databases can be searched by police force and by date, allowing you to tailor the data set to your research question(s).

As well as police arrest and stop and search data, statistics are also published regarding the characteristics of police officers. The Home Office publishes police workforce data that can be used to explore the number of police officers and police staff in various ranks, the gender and ethnicity of police officers and staff, and length of career, as well as statistics on police misconduct. These data sets provide a great resource for exploring the make-up of police forces in England and Wales.

Sentencing and Court Data

The Ministry of Justice (MoJ) collects and publishes data from the courts in England and Wales which can be accessed at gov.uk. The range of data sets you can access includes:

- Criminal court statistics
- Family court statistics
- Judiciary statistics
- Legal aid statistics
- Youth justice statistics

In England and Wales, the Crown Court Sentencing Survey (CCSS) was undertaken between 2010 and 2015 to explore sentence decision-making by judges. This data offers opportunities to explore what factors impacted on sentence decision-making. If you are undertaking research on the Scottish courts, you can access the Criminal Proceedings in Scotland Data. Data for Northern Ireland can be accessed from NI Courts and Tribunals Service Statistics. There are also excellent historical data sites if you are interested in historical sentencing and court data, such as the Proceedings of the Old Bailey 1674–1913, whereby you can generate your own quantitative data using the search facility.

Accessing such data enables you to undertake a range of possible studies, such as the number of cases going to court, the efficiency of the courts, and the demographics of people appearing in court. These statistics can also be analysed alongside policing statistics to compare arrest and prosecution data. If you are interested in courts and prosecution, it is worthwhile exploring what data is available to help shape the focus for your dissertation.

Prison and Probation Data

Prison and parole statistics from England and Wales are published by the MoJ, National Offender Management Service (NOMS) and Her Majesty's Prison and Probation Service (HMPPS). There is an abundance of data available to explore a range of topics including prisoner populations, prison performance and reoffending statistics.

Accessing prisons can be very problematic at undergraduate level, and some higher education institutions do not allow students to access prisons to undertake their dissertation projects. As discussed in Chapter 3, prisons have a duty of care towards prisoners, who are considered a vulnerable population, and a duty of care towards any researchers within the prison. The risk of harm to either prisoners or you is what prevents these institutions being accessible. This lack of access can lead students to choose to do a library-based piece of work on prisons. However, there is prison data available that you can utilise for your research without breaching ethical regulations. HM Inspectorate of Prisons undertakes surveys of prisoners and staff as part of its prison inspections. The results of the surveys can be downloaded from the HMI Prisons website (see Table 5.1), allowing you to analyse individual prisons and make comparisons across prisons. HMPPS also publishes data sets on equalities among its prison population that include data on gender, ethnicity, religion, and sexuality, allowing you to explore relationships between social characteristics of people in prison. If you are interested in exploring the data collected from prisons, you can explore the different topics and data sets available through gov.uk.

If you are interested in statistics on reoffending, these are published quarterly by the MoJ and enable you to explore statistical trends. Alongside the proven reoffending statistics is the Justice Data Lab, which publishes data on the impact of rehabilitation programmes. These are just some examples of data sets that are available at your disposal if you want to undertake statistical research on prisons, probation, and/or reoffending.

The prison and reconviction data for Scotland is published by the Scottish Government (under crime and justice statistics; link in Table 5.1). Scotland does not have a probation service; instead, it has a criminal justice social work service, which publishes statistical data on probation, community penalties, and community supervision.

Table 5.1 Links To Crime and Justice Statistical Data Sets

Resource	Where to Access
Office for National Statistics (Crime and Justice)	www.ons.gov.uk/ peoplepopulationandcommunity/ crimeandjustice
UK Data Service	www.ukdataservice.ac.uk
Crime Survey for England and Wales	www.crimesurvey.co.uk/en/index.html
Scottish Crime and Victimisation Survey	www.gov.scot/collections/ scottish-crime-and-justice-survey/
The Northern Ireland Safe Community Survey	www.justice-ni.gov.uk/topics/statistics-and-research/northern-ireland-safe-community-survey
Longitudinal Analysis of the Offending, Crime and Justice Survey	https://natcen.ac.uk/our-research/ research/longitudinal-analysis-of-the-offending-crime-and-justice-survey/
Data.Police.UK	https://data.police.uk/data/
Ministry of Justice Statistics	www.gov.uk/government/organisations/ ministry-of-justice/about/statistics
Crime and Justice Statistics Scotland	www.gov.scot/collections/ crime-and-justice-statistics/
Crime and Justice Statistics Northern Ireland	www.nisra.gov.uk/statistics/ crime-and-justice
HM Inspectorates of Prisons: reports	www.justiceinspectorates.gov.uk/ hmiprisons/inspections/
Proceedings of the Old Bailey 1697–1913	www.oldbaileyonline.org/
Crime Data America	www.icpsr.umich.edu and https://osf.io/ zyaqn/wiki/home/

Box 5.2 Using Existing Criminal Justice Institutional Data

Example 1: Gender and Policing

Kas is interested in whether the Gender Agenda policies have made a difference to the number of women entering and progressing in police forces in England. Kas is able to download the police workforce data and undertake a longitudinal analysis to determine whether there has been a change in the number of women joining the police and whether there are more women in senior police positions.

Example 2: Guilty Pleas and Sentencing

Billie wants to investigate the relationship between guilty pleas and sentencing decisions. Utilising the Crown Court Sentencing Survey (2015), Billie is able to undertake a comparison of sentences for individuals who did and did not plead guilty.

Example 3: Safety in Prison

Cameron is wanting to explore how safe prisoners feel in different prison categories. Cameron is able to utilise the prisoner surveys undertaken as part of the inspection reports to compare how safe prisoners feel across a sample of category A, B, C, and D male prisons.

Existing Qualitative Data

The chapter so far has outlined a range of quantitative data sources that you can freely access, download, and undertake your own statistical analysis on. This section of the chapter outlines existing qualitative data that can be used for dissertations by discussing different types of documents you can access and analyse using qualitative methods. A list of resources that are discussed and relevant links to access them can be found in Table 5.2 at the end of this section.

Qualitative Data Sets

The Economic and Social Research Council (ESRC) established a resource centre called Qualidata in 1994 as a repository for qualitative researchers to make their data available for secondary data analysis. The qualitative data sets are now available through the UK Data Service and can be used to either reanalyse the data to answer a new research question or to reanalyse the data using the original research question but using a different perspective or theoretical framework. Utilising the existing qualitative data in such repositories can be a beneficial way to undertake a qualitative piece of work without the time, cost, access, and ethical barriers that are often presented. The types of qualitative data archived on the UK Data Service include interviews, focus groups, and observations. You can use the search functions to input keywords for your topic, the type of data you are looking for, or the date range and location, depending on what you are interested in.

While there are clear practical benefits of undertaking secondary qualitative analysis, the limitations of this method need be addressed. One limitation is the issue of not collecting the qualitative data yourself; qualitative data is, by its nature, subjective and relies on individual interpretations of the data. The context in which data is collected can be just as important as the data itself, so any endeavour to undertake secondary qualitative data analysis should ensure that the context is considered (see Wincup, 2017). There are also the ethical issues in relation to informed consent and anonymity, so before undertaking any secondary analysis, it is important to check whether the original research had ethical approval for the data to be reused.

Media Sources

Researching the media and crime is a popular choice among undergraduate criminology students, and contemporary media opens opportunities for students to undertake analysis of media in varying formats. The types of media sources that can be used include film and TV, social media, radio, music, poetry, comics and magazines, news and newspapers, and fictional books. The type of research you undertake can also vary, from a quantitative content analysis to a qualitative narrative analysis and even a visual analysis (see

Riffe et al., 1998; Moore, 2014; Brown, 2017). Box 5.3 provides three example dissertations published on the Internet Journal of Criminology that all utilised different media sources to address their research questions.

A commonly used media format for undergraduate students is news coverage, mainly newspaper stories of crime and criminal justice. The benefits of using newspapers and online news media are that they are free to access and can be used either as the sole method of data collection or combined with other methods. There are various ways of searching newspaper articles, but one of the most convenient is using LexisNexis, which is an archive of news items dating back to 1981. You can use many search features in LexisNexis to search for topics, keywords, dates, and regions, enabling you to narrow down your search to stories that are relevant to your research question(s). Researching the news can be used to explore representations of crime and criminal justice, crime narratives in the news, imagery in crime news, and news framing (see Example 2 in Box 5.3). You should also take account of the different news outlets' agendas, political affiliations, and target audience, because the nature and intentions of different publications will have a direct impact on any comparisons you undertake.

Film and television can be used to explore how crime and criminal justice is portrayed on screen. Undergraduate dissertations can explore cultural narratives, dominant ideologies (see Example 1 in Box 5.3), and visual representations using such sources. You can access film and TV through your own streaming services, or your institution may subscribe to a service such as Box of Broadcasts, which is an archive and streaming service of thousands of TV and radio shows. These media sources can also be combined with data from other research methods, such as focus groups, surveys, or interviews to ask people their perceptions of crime on TV and film.

Social media platforms can be used to collect data that has been published publicly online. You can undertake a range of difference analysis, from content and thematic analysis to social network and semantic analysis, depending on the platform you extract data from. Twitter is one such platform that has attracted a lot of research attention, with the facility to search for data using hashtags, follow live issues, or use it in combination with other methods (see Example 3 in Box 5.3). There are a range of different software programmes available, such as Chorus Analytics, if you want to undertake a large analysis of tweets, but you can also undertake your own searches and create a sampling method to use as your own data set. Other virtual documents such as blogs, chat rooms, and websites can be used as sources of data, but careful consideration needs to be given to the ethical issues associated with accessing and using such data (see Bryman, 2016; Wall and Williams, 2011; Wincup, 2017).

Box 5.3 Examples of Student Dissertations Using Media Sources

Example 1: *"I Hope Boris Johnson Watches Top Boy"*: *A Synthetic and Critical Analysis of Popular Culture*

In this dissertation, McDonnell (2020) undertook a critical analysis of the representation of young black males in the TV show *Top Boy*. The dissertation explored the dominant ideologies in this TV show using a critical discourse analysis and argued that even a fictional TV show can raise important social and political issues that affect the lives of young black men.

Example 2: *Constructing the Perfect Terrorist Attack: Critical Evaluation of News Values and Media Representations*

Ralph (2016) used the framework of newsworthiness to explore whether it could be applied to the way in which UK news media portrayed terrorist attacks. Using two terror attack case studies, Ralph sampled a cross section of stories from three UK newspapers and BBC news coverage. The dissertation was able to demonstrate the difficulties of applying the theory of newsworthiness to stories of terrorism and the importance of other factors that impact on the way a story is told.

Example 3: *To What Extent Is Sexual Assault Occurring in the Night-Time Economy Normalised?*

In this dissertation, Cashman (2019) used a mixed methods approach that consisted of a survey and a non-participant observation of tweets from the #MeToo movement. A thematic analysis of 100 sample tweets was undertaken to compare with a survey Cashman had undertaken. The dissertation was able to gain a more in-depth understanding of perceptions of sexual assault by using both a survey sample and a wider sample from Twitter.

Historical Data

Archived data enables you to get a glimpse into the past and explore historical crimes, historical criminal justice proceedings, portrayals of crime, and personal documents that detail experiences of crime. There are many different archives that you can access either freely or through your university subscriptions. The John Johnson Collection has thousands of documents that you can search through– everything from trial proceedings and prisoner records to crime narratives, posters, and news articles. There are also archives of execution ballads that can be found on the Broadside Ballads and Execution Ballads websites, which are open access (weblinks listed in Table 5.2). The Digital Panopticon is a historical resource dedicated to providing historical records on crime and criminal justice from 1780 to 1925. It contains records and life course information of people sentenced at the Old Bailey and is an excellent resource for gaining an insight

Table 5.2 Qualitative Data Sources

Resource	Where to Access
UK Data Service	www.ukdataservice.ac.uk
LexisNexis*	www.lexisnexis.com/uk/legal/news?sourceid=1061905
Box of Broadcasts*	https://learningonscreen.ac.uk/ondemand
Chorus Analytics	http://chorusanalytics.co.uk/
The John Johnson Collection	http://johnjohnson.chadwyck.co.uk/home.do
Execution Ballads	https://omeka.cloud.unimelb.edu.au/execution-ballads/
	http://ballads.bodleian.ox.ac.uk/
Digital Panopticon	www.digitalpanopticon.org/
The National Archives	www.nationalarchives.gov.uk/help-with-your-research/research-guides/crime-and-punishment/
Parliamentary Papers Archive	https://parlipapers.proquest.com/

*You may need to access these through your institution's subscription.

into trials, punishments, and offender characteristics during that time period.

Digital archives, such as those mentioned, provide a free and accessible way to access secondary data to undertake your own qualitative analysis. There are also options to access hard-copy police, crime and court data from the local and national archives; however, this type of access can be more time-consuming than accessing data that is available digitally. Your institution may also subscribe to the House of Commons Parliamentary Papers, which is an archive of UK parliamentary bills and papers dating back to 1688. Historical legislation can be used to understand how legislation on crime and justice has evolved in the UK or can be used for comparative analysis (see Example 2 in Box 5.4). For further discussion on using historical records, see Cox, Shore and Godfrey (2018) and Noaks and Wincup (2004, Chapter 7).

The digitisation of historical data makes it a great resource if you have an interest in the history of crime and justice. It is always worth exploring what historical databases your institution subscribes to, as there are many newspaper archives, visual archives, and book archives available online. Your academic librarian would be able to help with any questions you have about these.

Official and Unofficial Documents

Government policy and legislative documents can be a great source of secondary data for exploring a range of crime and justice topics. The documents can be used in isolation to explore the narratives and discourses of official policy and legislation, but policy document analysis can also be used in combination with other empirical methods to establish whether policies are followed in situational practice (see Example 3 in Box 5.4). All criminal justice institutions have a range of legislations and policies they are expected to follow, and they can provide an insight into how such organisations have changed over time and what the core narratives are in criminal justice policy. It is beyond the scope of this text to cover all the legislation and various organisational policies; however, these are easily accessed online. For example, all legislation in the UK can be found at www.legislation.gov.uk/. Policies, published guidelines (such as the sentencing guidelines) and legislation should be treated as sources of qualitative text data. However, when using such data (as with any other secondary source), caution needs to be given to the credibility of the sources and any underlying biases they represent. Before undertaking any research involving analysis of official documents, it would be worthwhile understanding their strengths and limitations by understanding the context in which they were written and who they were written by.

Other documents that can be utilised as secondary sources include organisational data (such as briefing reports, inspection reports, and mission statements), personal documents (such as diaries, journals, and letters), and visual documents (posters, photographs, and advertising). Any form of published document can be utilised for secondary analysis; however, you must always check the permissions associated with such documents (especially personal documents).

If you are collecting data that does not come from human participants, such as policy documents, websites, newspapers, and/or images, you still need to devise a **sampling strategy** to determine what you will collect and how much of the source(s) to collect. For example, if you are undertaking an analysis of prison inspection reports, you will need to decide what sample to include in your analysis. Setting criteria – such as what type of prison (open/closed, high/low security, male/female), when the inspections were undertaken, and what factors you will be using in the analysis – will enable you to create a sample for analysis. The same approach applies for media analysis, whereby you should set criteria to sample an appropriate number of sources for analysis. Ralph (2016) discusses in their dissertation how they created sampling criteria for 20 newspaper articles by narrowing down the stories, timescale, and types of newspapers to include in the analysis. Creating a sampling strategy will enable you to exclude resources that are less relevant, saving time and ensuring you do not get overwhelmed with data.

Box 5.4 Examples of Student Dissertations Using Policy and Historical Data

Example 1: *The EU Plan of Action on Combating Terrorism: an Ambiguous and Redundant Tool of Governance*

Delaney's (2013) dissertation provides a good example of undertaking a thematic analysis of legislative data. It compares the theories of counter-terrorism with the EU plan to combat terrorism. Delaney's research was able to draw conclusions as to the effectiveness of the plan against what the literature tells us on effective counter-terrorism.

Example 2 (mock): *The Aliens Act 1905: To What Extent Has the Narrative Changed?*

Frankie's dissertation is exploring a comparative narrative analysis between the 1905 Aliens Act and the Immigration Act 2016. Frankie can access the Aliens Act 1905 from the Parliamentary Papers archive and the Immigration Act 2016 from the UK legislation website. Frankie analyses the narratives in both pieces of legislation to explore whether there have been any changes to the manner in which immigrants are referred to in UK legislation.

Example 3 (mock): *The Role of Risk in Parole Decision-Making*

Mel undertakes a dissertation on risk in the criminal justice system. They undertake a document analysis of the Parole Process Policy Framework (2020) and the Parole Board Decision-Making Framework (2019) to assess how the discourse of risk is used within these policies. Mel also undertakes semi-structured interviews with parole board members to discuss the role of risk in their decision-making. This dissertation is able to utilise the policies to explore how they are interpreted and followed in practice.

This section has demonstrated the variety of resources you can access to undertake qualitative data analysis on existing data. Whether you are interested in history, the media, policy and legislation, or accessing empirical research project data, it is worthwhile exploring the different archives and data sets available to you. There are clear benefits of using pre-existing data, in terms of both ethics and practicalities, but you must also ensure the data is suitable for the type of project you are undertaking. Even if you decide to collect your own qualitative data, it is important to remember that resources such as those discussed in this section can be used in conjunction with other methods in your dissertation.

Summary and Checklist

This chapter has introduced you to some of the key resources you can use to access secondary data. Further guidance on undertaking research using secondary sources can be found in a range of research texts; some suggestions are provided at the end of this chapter. The chapter has discussed the benefits of different types of qualitative and quantitative data and provided examples of how such resources could be used for a dissertation. This chapter has not provided an exhaustive list of resources, but it provides a starting point for exploring the range of resources available to you. Before moving on to the next chapter, it is worthwhile completing the chapter checklist in Box 5.5.

Box 5.5 Checklist

1   Are there possible data sets you could use to answer
    your research question(s)?   ☐
2   What data sets would be most beneficial to your
    dissertations?   ☐
3   Is there data already out there that could complement
    data you intend to collect yourself?   ☐
4   Would utilising secondary data help you overcome
    ethical issues in your dissertation?   ☐
5   Are you able to identify the benefits and limitations
    of using secondary data?   ☐

Further Reading

Bryman, A. (2016) *Social Research Methods.* 5th edn. Oxford: Oxford University Press. Chapter 14.

Matthews, B. and Ross, L. (2010) *Research Methods.* Harlow: Pearson. Chapter 9.

Wincup, E. (2017) *Criminological Research: Understanding Qualitative Methods.* 2nd edn. London: Sage. Chapter 5.

Chapter 6

Collecting Primary Data

Overview

It is expected that you will have already undertaken a module/course in research methods as part of your degree to date and will have a good understanding of different methods of data collection and analysis. This chapter aims to provide guidance if you intend to collect primary data for your dissertation, discussing some of the obstacles students can face and the practicalities that require consideration. It outlines the key stages of undertaking primary data collection, offers suggested activities to assist you in the process, and discusses some key issues you may face.

By the end of this chapter you should:

- Understand the benefits and limitations of collecting primary data
- Be familiar with the design and sampling considerations for primary research
- Be familiar with common issues that can arise during the data collection process

Advantages of Collecting Primary Data

Chapter 4 discussed the range of existing data that can be utilised in a dissertation. However, the data you require to answer your question may not exist in any data set, so you may need to collect your own. Generating your own data for analysis in a dissertation, if it is ethically possible to do so, has many benefits. The first benefit is that it enables you to demonstrate advanced research skills: designing research questions, devising a data collection strategy, undertaking data analysis,

DOI: 10.4324/9781003016335-7

and inferring conclusions from your own data. It provides you with an opportunity to design a truly unique piece of research that you can take ownership of.

It can also be a beneficial way to contribute to knowledge if there is little empirical work undertaken on the chosen topic, or if large methodological gaps exist in your area of study. Instead of having to design a research question around what data is available, you can design a study specific to your areas of interest and directly relevant to your research question(s). A final benefit of undertaking this type of dissertation is the practical skills you develop by collecting your own data, which are core transferable skills.

Limitations of Collecting Primary Data

There are always going to be limitations to any dissertation, and it is important to consider whether the benefits outweigh the limitations before commencing with an empirical study. Each research method has its own limitations; you should be familiar with these from your research methods modules, so this will not be discussed in detail here. Instead, we will consider limitations in relation to data collection in your dissertation.

The first limitation relates to your own skill set. While you may want to carry out your own data collection (whether it be observations, surveys, or interviews), you should first consider whether you have the necessary skills to do so. Learning about different research methods is very different from doing research in practice. You will know what your skills are and whether you are equipped to undertake your own research. Designing surveys, undertaking interviews, and taking observational notes all require skill, and you need to be confident you have the skills before you embark on the research. This is not to say that you cannot undertake your own data collection if you are a novice, but rather you need to factor these limitations in and consider the impact they would have on the quality of the data you gather.

Time and resources are limitations that you need to consider from the outset of your dissertation. The time to complete a dissertation can range from 6 to 10 months depending on your institution's term times. The short time to undertake a research project requires careful planning and being realistic about what you can achieve. This will have a bearing on your target population and sample size, so it is advisable you acknowledge that the data you collect may be affected in quantity and/or quality as a result. You should also spend time scoping out the feasibility of your study: do you have access to the resources that you will need to undertake the fieldwork? Will there be costs involved, or access restrictions? Ensuring the resources are available before committing to primary data collection is important.

The remainder of this chapter will discuss the different steps involved in planning and undertaking primary data collection, and what challenges you need to address.

Designing Your Data Collection Approach

If you have decided that collecting primary data is the most appropriate method to answer your research question, and will be ethically feasible, you should start designing the data collection strategy as soon as possible. The method you choose should be determined by your research question and epistemological stance. The first thing to consider is what sort of data you will need to answer your research question, what depth of information you will need, and whether the data you collect will be able to answer your question. For example, a closed-question survey is unlikely to provide you with in-depth details about people's perceptions or experiences. Similarly, small-scale, in-depth interviews will not provide you with quantifiable data to explore large-scale trends. The wording of your research question will be a good indicator of what type of data you will need to collect. Have a go at the two activities in Box 6.1; if you need to refresh your knowledge on the relationship between ontology, epistemology and methodology, please look at Caulfield and Hill (2018, Chapter 6), listed in the further reading.

Once you have established what type of question you are asking and what type of data you need to collect, you can start exploring different methods that would be most appropriate to use. For instance, if you have decided that you will be undertaking a qualitative project, what type of qualitative data will you collect? This could be interviews or focus groups, letters or diaries, images, or observations. Smith et al. (2009: 70) provide a nice summary of the benefits and limitations of different research methods; it would be worthwhile noting down what the advantages and disadvantages of your chosen methods are and taking time to explore possible alternatives.

Box 6.1   Student Activity 9

Activity 9: Designing Your Data Collection Method

1 **Look at the different research questions below and decide what would be the best methodological approach and method(s):**

a   To what extent does household income relate to crime victimisation?

b   Do individuals from low-income households experience victimisation differently from those in high-income households?

2. **Create a table with your research question, like the one below:**

	Example 1: Measuring attitudes towards knife crime	*Example 2: People's experiences of being a witness in court*	*Your research question*
Ontology	objective	constructivist	
Epistemology	positive	interpretivist	
Methodology	quantitative	qualitative	
Method	questionnaire	interviews	

Designing the Research Tool

Whether you intend to undertake observations, facilitate focus groups, or distribute an online survey, you will be required to create a research tool, such as an interview schedule or structured questionnaire. For many, this will be the first time you have been tasked with designing a tool to collect your own data, and it can be difficult to know where to start.

The first step is to consider carefully what information your research question is looking for and break that down into sub-questions; have a look at the example in Box 6.2, which is from Butters' (2021) undergraduate dissertation. Breaking down your own research question enables you to identify what aspects are most important.

Box 6.2 Example: Breaking Down Questions

Butters' (2021) dissertation explored the *Perceptions of the Use and Effectiveness of Victim Personal Statements within West Yorkshire Police.* To understand these perceptions, Butters broke down her research focus into four sub-questions:

- How is the VPS delivered by West Yorkshire Police?
- What is the understanding of interviewed officers of the purpose of VPS?
- How effective is the VPS scheme?
- What improvements are needed?

Once you have clear questions to focus on, you can start to design your research tool. It is beyond the scope of this text to go into depth on designing different tools; you can find guidance in the suggested further reading. However, you should consider the questions in Box 6.3 when you start designing the tool for your project.

Box 6.3 Top Tips: Designing Your Research Tool

- How structured will your tool be – does it require every participant to answer the same questions?
- Will you need open or closed questions, or a mixture of both?
- How will you order the questions? For instance, it is advisable to avoid opening a survey or interview with very personal questions.
- If undertaking some form of observation, what key things are you looking for?
- What language will you use? Take care to ensure you use accessible, non-leading language in your research tool.

It is always recommended that you pilot your research tool before commencing any fieldwork. Using a pilot survey or a pilot focus group/interview allows you to test out your research tool, ensuring it provides you with the data you need, and offers an opportunity to identify any issues in advance. A pilot is also beneficial for practising your skills (especially if you are facilitating a focus group or under-taking interviews for the first time); you can use it to get feedback on how you ask questions and whether participants understood what you were asking them. For further discussion on the benefit of pilot studies, please see Malmqvist et al. (2019) and Smith (2019).

Sampling and Recruitment

This is one of the most important decisions you must make when designing your data collection strategy. Who or what you sample, and how you sample, will have a large bearing on what data you are able to collect. Using your research question, you need to consider the following:

• Who/what do you need to sample to answer your research question?
• Do you have easy access to the people/resources you need to sample?
• How many people/resources will you need to sample?

There are various sampling strategies that you can choose from, and your research objectives will determine what sampling strategy best suits your project (e.g., random versus purposive sampling), whether you need to create a sampling frame, and how large your sample needs to be for validity and reliability (see Matthews and Ross, 2010: 152–173 for further discussions on sampling). However, a balance is often needed between what the ideal sample is and what a realistic sample for a dissertation is likely to be.

Let's begin by considering sample sizes– because the larger your sample size, the more data you must analyse for your dissertation. It is common for students to propose very large sample sizes at the start of their dissertation, but a large sample size is not always needed or achievable. The time you have available to collect and analyse data means that it may not be possible to recruit large samples. As a guide, I always suggest that students aim for around the following when recruiting people to participate:

• Six to ten participants for a semi-structured interview
• Two focus groups (four to six people in each)
• 50 participants for a questionnaire/survey

The variation in sample size will depend on many factors, and you should not let it deter you from your chosen method. For example, many qualitative projects that undertake semi-structured interviews use purposive sampling due to the participant criteria put in place. Narrow criteria will lead to smaller samples, but that does not make the data any less meaningful. If you look at the dissertations by Nash (2019) and Jacklin (2020), both students interviewed three participants for their study, while Chamberlain (2019) interviewed six participants, and Butters (2021) interviewed seven. The same can be seen in survey research, which again can be difficult to recruit for. Toomey (2019) distributed an online survey to 45 participants and received 26 responses, whereas Cashman (2019) distributed an online survey in the hope of recruiting 100 participants but ended up with 167 responses. It is imperative that you keep in mind the time restrictions you are under during your dissertation and that you are realistic about how many people you will be able to recruit and collect data from, and how long it will take to analyse the data collected. If you end up recruiting fewer people than you had initially planned for, then do not be too concerned. All dissertations have limitations in some way or another; the important thing is what you do with the data once you collect it. Any limitations can be discussed in your methodology chapter (see Chapter 7 of this text).

Once you have decided on your target population to sample and your sampling strategy, your next task is to recruit people to your study. How you advertise your research and recruit participants will depend on your individual project, the criteria you have devised for participants, and any access restrictions. It is beyond the scope of this chapter to go through every possible way to recruit participants; however, Table 6.1 offers some benefits and limitations of different recruitment methods. It is important to remember that you must put the work in when recruiting people to participate and you may need to adopt several strategies until you get the desired sample.

Collecting Your Data

Collecting your own data will involve careful planning and time management. I recommend you read up on the benefits, limitations, and practicalities of different methods of data collection before committing to an approach (e.g., Caulfield and Hill, 2018: 155–205 and Jenson and

Table 6.1 Recruiting Participants

Type of recruitment	Benefits	Limitations
Email/telephone invitations	Only those who fit the criteria will be invited Offer a personal invitation	Requires you to have people's contact details Need to ensure email/telephone invitations are clear as to why potential participants are receiving them
Advertise through social media	Large audience Good for snowballing	Not everyone will use social media Need to ensure you use the most appropriate social media platform for target audience
Posters	Can be visually effective Relatively straightforward to create and distribute	Low recruitment method Target population may not see them
Through gatekeepers	Access to relevant participants	Reliant on gatekeepers in terms of their time and trustworthiness to recruit on your behalf

Laurie, 2016: 135–220). However, there are some key considerations to make no matter what type of data you are collecting that this section will cover.

The first consideration to make is **time** – how much time you can spend collecting your data. It is likely that you will be studying other modules while undertaking your dissertation, and you may also have work, family, or caring responsibilities that need to be considered when planning your data collection. A further consideration is how much time you have before your dissertation deadline. It is important to remember that the analysis and writing up of your research findings need a considerable amount of time, so it is best to avoid leaving these stages too late.

If you are undertaking an online survey, for example, you need to set a cut-off date for when the survey will close. You will want to allow participants enough time to respond and complete your survey, but you also need to be mindful of when you will want to start the analysis. The activity in Box 6.4 gives you examples of how to make time considerations for your data collection.

Box 6.4 Student Activity 10

Activity 10: Time Planning for Data Collection

Create a plan for fieldwork to help you identify a realistic timeframe for collecting data. Consider the following when doing this:

• Personal commitments
• Deadline for dissertation
• Other course deadlines
• The time needed to collect the data

The examples below give suggestions of how you could create your own plan for data collection by thinking through just how long the collection might take.

Example	Considerations
Collecting eight semi-structured interviews	Each interview to last one hour Travel time before and after interview: 30 minutes Reflecting and note taking after each interview: one hour = 20 hours minimum to collect the data
Collecting online surveys	Dissertation deadline in 12 weeks Require four weeks to input and analyse data Require four weeks to write up findings Require two weeks to finish and present dissertation correctly = two weeks maximum to collect the data
Analysing five × two-hour TV documentaries	Time to watch and rewatch each documentary/episode: 20 hours Time to take notes during and after watching: ten hours = 30 hours minimum to collect the data

---

The next consideration to make is **data storage**, both for ethical reasons and for organisational purposes. While you are collecting data you need to decide how you are going to store that data, and this is particularly important when collecting data from human participants. You need to abide by data protection legislation and take great care to ensure research data is stored correctly. You should consult your university's data protection policy before collecting data to ensure you are familiar with the processes. These will normally advise on what storage is deemed to be secure, how to back up data securely, and how to encrypt data. If you are doing research within an organisation, they may have their own requirements for data storage that you should check before collecting data. Even if you are not collecting data considered to be confidential, you still need to ensure you keep your data organised and safe, so you do not run the risk of losing either parts or all your data. Have a look at the activity in Box 6.5 and consider what might be problematic with each scenario and how to prevent the issues from occurring.

Box 6.5   Student Activity 11

Activity 11: Data Storage

Have a look at the scenarios below and consider:

- What are the problems with their data storage methods?
- What should they do?

Example 1

Bev is undertaking interviews for her dissertation. She decides to record the interviews so she can transcribe and analyse them at a later date. Bev uses her mobile phone to record the interviews; she deems this a secure method, because her phone is password protected.

Example 2

Will has collected online surveys and has exported the data to a shared laptop. To ensure nobody else can access the data, Will downloads the data onto a memory stick and then deletes it from the shared laptop.

Example 3

Aaron is undertaking an observation of campus security officers. He is shadowing the officers while taking handwritten notes. All the notes are in a dedicated notebook that he stores in his backpack, and he keeps the backpack in his university flat while he is not using it.

The final thing to consider is what to do if things do not go to plan. It is very common in all research projects that data collection does not go as planned. This can happen for a variety of reasons, including access being blocked at the last minute, not getting enough participants, interviews being too short, or not being able to find resources. The first piece of advice is not to panic: problems during the data collection stage are all part of the research process. If you had set out to undertake eight interviews but only ended up with three participants, or had aimed to collect 50 surveys but only received 20 responses, then do not worry. The important thing is what you do with the data you have collected, and that you acknowledge the problems when writing up your methodology chapter (see Chapter 7 of this text for further discussion). If you start collecting data and realise that you need to change something, such as your research tool or sample, then discuss this with your supervisor. If it is early enough in the process, you can use the initial responses as your pilot, learn from the mistakes, and start the data collection over. If it is late in the process, then discuss with your supervisor what the issues are; the chances are the data collection is not wasted, and whatever you have collected will have value for your dissertation.

There are always difficulties when undertaking a dissertation, and students undertaking empirical projects will encounter a range of obstacles in the process; this is entirely normal and to be expected. Conducting your own empirical study for the first time can be a steep learning curve, and with that will come mistakes that you can learn from. Different types of research come with different problems and one way to ensure these do not have a detrimental impact on your study is to anticipate them in advance. Use the activity in Box 6.6 to help you identify and mitigate against potential problems that may arise.

Box 6.6 Student Activity 12

Activity 12: Anticipating Problems

Create a table, like the one below, to note down what problems you may encounter during your data collection and consider possible solutions. A couple of examples have been provided for you. Discuss your potential problems with your supervisor before commencing your field work.

Example potential problem	Why is it a problem	What are the consequences	Are there any skills I need to develop to mitigate against it	What to do if this does happen
Not enough survey responses	Impact on validity and reliability of findings	Research conclusions will be limited	Learn different strategies for recruiting participants	Acknowledge the limitation of findings in the dissertation
Participants not saying much in interviews	The data is not in any depth and limited in content	The data does not answer the research question	Interviewing skills to learn how to probe for further information/ follow up on answers given	Revisit the interview schedule, ensure there are open ended and probing questions

Summary and Checklist

This chapter has covered key considerations you need to make when planning to undertake a dissertation that involves collecting primary data. The chapter has covered the processes required, the obstacles you may come across, and some strategies for ensuring you can successfully collect the data. Use the checklist in Box 6.7 to help you manage your data collection process.

Box 6.7 Checklist

1 Chosen a methodological approach that aligns with your research question(s) ☐
2 Ensured you have the required skills to undertake the project ☐
3 Identified a sample that is reachable and realistic for a dissertation ☐
4 Designed an effective method of recruiting participants ☐
5 Designed and piloted your research tool ☐
6 Completed a time management plan ☐
7 Checked the data protection requirements for your research ☐
8 Completed Activities 9–12 ☐

Further Reading

Caufield, L.S. and Hill, J. (2018) *Criminological Skills and research for Beginners.* 2nd edn. London: Routledge. Chapter 6.

Jensen, E.A. and Laurie, C. (2016) *Doing Real Research.* London: Sage. Chapters 7 and 8.

Matthews, B. and Ross, L. (2010) *Research Methods: A Practical Guide for the Social Sciences.* Essex: Pearson. Part C.

Chapter 7

Writing a Methodology Chapter

Overview

This chapter will offer you guidance on writing a methodology chapter for your dissertation. All research projects need to outline clearly what was undertaken and why, no matter whether the dissertation is library-based or empirical. This chapter will outline what should be included in your methodology discussion and offer suggestions for structuring it, according to the different types of dissertations.

By the end of this chapter you should:

- Understand the importance of outlining your methodology
- Understand the key components of a methodology chapter
- Understand how to structure a methodology chapter

The Importance of a Methodology Chapter

All dissertations in criminology are research projects, whereby you set a research question and use evidence to answer it. How you answer that question will depend on what approach you choose, whether that be library-based, secondary data analysis, or primary data analysis. It is therefore important that all dissertations include a discussion of **what** you did, **how** you did it and **why** you chose that approach. All published research includes a section that discusses methodology. Have a look at research reports, journal articles, and monographs, and you will see a section somewhere that discusses how the research was undertaken. Including a discussion of your methodology has two key benefits. This first is that it enables your readers to understand the process you undertook to answer your research question, meaning that

DOI: 10.4324/9781003016335-8

the quality of the study, in terms of its rigour and reliability, can easily be evaluated. The second benefit is that it allows you to demonstrate your knowledge and understanding of research methods and showcase the skills you have developed.

Methodology Chapters in Library-Based Dissertations

A question most supervisors get asked is "Do I need a methodology chapter if I am doing a library-based dissertation?" The simple answer is yes: ideally, you should be including a discussion of how you undertook your library-based dissertation. Remember from Chapter 1 of this text that a library-based project is still considered research; the difference is that you are using already published material to answer a research question. In essence, your sample and your data are the existing literature, and therefore you need to demonstrate how you identified and selected the literature that is included in your dissertation.

The aim of a library-based dissertation is to scrutinise existing literature to answer your research question(s). Your topic and research question will have determined what approach you used; for instance, you may have undertaken a systematic review of existing research (either meta-analysis or metasynthesis), a theoretical review of existing work to explore the application of relevant theories and concepts, or an integrative review of literature that brings together different bodies of work to generate new perspectives and/or frameworks. It is important that whoever reads your dissertation understands how you undertook your evaluation/analysis of existing literature to answer your research question.

In a library-based dissertation, your methodology (i.e., the approach you have chosen to answer your question) needs to be outlined clearly to your reader, although it is expected this methodology discussion will be shorter than you would typically find in an empirical project. The library-based dissertations of Heslop (2019) and Scott (2019) offer very good examples of writing a methodology for your library-based project. Heslop sets out nicely why the library-based approach was used and how they collated sources to be included, as well as identifying the limitations. Scott (2019) offers a justification for their approach to analysing existing literature. Both examples showcase the students' knowledge and application of research methods.

The methodology chapter in a library-based project is typically found either after the introductory chapter or after the literature review, depending on how you have set out your dissertation. Box 7.1 outlines what you should include in your methodology discussion.

Box 7.1 Top Tips: Components of a Methodology Chapter in Library-Based Dissertations

Your methodology chapter should include a discussion of the following:

- Rationale for choosing a library-based project
- Your methodological approach
- Methods employed to sample relevant literature
- How you evaluated and/or analysed existing literature
- Any limitations or further considerations

Methodology Chapters in Secondary and Primary Data Analysis

If you are undertaking a secondary data analysis, such as those discussed in Chapter 5 of this text, or have chosen to collect your own data, as discussed in Chapter 6, you will need to dedicate a chapter of your dissertation to your methodology. The chapter should be a discussion of what you did, with clear rationales that demonstrate your understanding of research methods. The methodology chapter should follow on nicely from your literature review, which will have ended with a clear focus for the research and an outline of how your research will add to existing literature. The methodology section then sets out what you did to undertake your research.

The chapter will have to cover what approach you took, the method(s) employed, sampling, analysis, and ethics. For each of these, a justification, using research methods literature, needs to be provided. It is also suggested that you include some reflections in your methodology chapter discussing how the process went, any difficulties that arose or limitations to your data collection. A suggested structure for a methodology chapter is provided in Box 7.2; however, you should discuss the structure of your chapter with your supervisor, who may prefer an alternative approach.

Box 7.2 Example: Suggested Structure of a Methodology Chapter for Empirical Projects

Introduction

- Introduce what the chapter will cover
- Restate your research question(s) and key objectives

Methodological Approach

- Describe what approach you took and why (ontology/epistemology/methodology)
- Discuss why other approaches were not suitable
- Ensure your methodological approach fits with the research question(s)

Method(s)

- State what method(s) you employed to undertake your research
- Discuss why it was the most suitable method
- Explain why other methods were less appropriate

Sample

- Outline clearly who or what was sampled
- Discuss your sampling strategy and sampling frames (if you used them) and sampling criteria
- Discuss your sample size
- Discuss how you undertook your sampling
- Discuss any limitations to your sampling strategy (i.e., reliability and validity)

Data Collection*

- Discuss how your data was collected
- Give precise details, such as: length of interviews, how many surveys were collected, how you collected content from documents, how long the data collection process took
- Reflect on any difficulties during the data collection stage

Data Analysis

- Outline your method of data analysis and why you chose that method
- Describe what you did with the data after you collected it and how you organised it; explain how you drew key findings from it
- Discuss the advantages and disadvantages of the analysis method you chose
- Include any personal reflections on how you analysed your data

Ethics

- Discuss the key ethical issues associated with your project
- Discuss how you ensured your project met ethical guidelines (including data protection)
- Even if your project had minimal ethical issues, you should state why this was the case

Chapter Summary

- You should end your chapter by summarising your methodology and signposting your reader to the next chapter

★ *Some projects will not require this section; for example, if you are using a downloaded data set.*

Your reader should have a very clear picture of all the steps you performed to undertake your research, be able to judge the reliability and validity of your study, and be confident that you understand the key benefits and limitations of different research methods. No empirical project is ever perfect, but by offering a clear description of what you did and why you did it, while acknowledging the limitations, you will ensure you have a robust methodology chapter. Have a look at some methodology chapter extracts in Box 7.3 which help to illustrate how justifications should be built into your discussions.

Box 7.3 Example Methodological Justifications in Empirical Projects

Justifying the Methodological Approach: Cashmore (2017:13)

This research requires a relative ontological analysis with an emic epistemological approach. Relative ontology recognises that what CPOs [community protection officers] are and do, and whether they have met expectations, is not an absolute truth. Instead, this understanding is shaped by the experiences and changing perspectives of each participant (Killam, 2013). To discover what the context for these perspectives, it is necessary to adopt an emic epistemological method, wherein the researcher must understand that the opinions and expectations of participants are shaped by their subjective knowledge and experiences (ibid.).

Justifying the Research Method: Butters (2021: 23)

Qualitative research has its limitations. Firstly, the results of the data collected will not be generalisable. Qualitative data is not usually conducted using representative samples (Wincup, 2017) and that is true of this study. As a result, the findings can't be used to assume the views, attitudes and opinions of the wider police force of England and Wales or even West Yorkshire Police as a whole. Secondly, replication will not be possible. The researcher is the main instrument of data collection and brings along "his or her own preferences" (Bryman, 2016, p398) … [Q]ualitative data collection is by its nature subjective. However, these are limitations of the qualitative approach not of this research and despite them, it is an approach which is best suited to this study. "Qualitative interviews are best suited to projects which aim to understand the perspectives of interviewees and what is important to them" (Wincup, 2017 p98). It is the perspective of West Yorkshire Officers to the Victim Personal Statement this research is interested in.

Justifying the Sampling Method: Harrop (2019: 19)

As the study is not calling for a specific professional group, the researcher felt that a convenience sample would be a suitable approach for this study. In essence, a convenience sample involves the selection of research participants because of their availability to the researcher. The use of convenience sampling is typically a favoured approach in purposive sampling because of its aid in overcoming barriers to research, given that it is both cost and time effective (Taherdoost, 2016). Whilst the use of convenience sampling allows an ease to conducting research, a major disadvantage is that researchers are unable to claim that their findings are representative of a population (Etikan et al., 2015). Although the researcher acknowledges this limitation, the strengths in convenience sampling for this study is based on the assessment that this type of method provides an appropriate starting point for a study where little research exists (Loiselle et al., 2010).

Preparing to Write Your Methodology Chapter

A methodology chapter is one that can be worked on throughout the dissertation process and does not need to be left until the end. A good approach to take that makes writing your methodology chapter easier is to use your **research diary** (see Box 1.3 in Chapter 1); this will help you keep note of everything you did, how long different stages took, and any problems you faced, and provides the chance to note down your personal reflections during each stage. For every decision you make, you should note in your research diary why you made that decision. Consider, for instance, why you chose an online rather than a paper survey, or why you opted for interviews over focus groups. The more you keep note of during the research process, the easier it is to compile your methodology chapter. You can start drafting the different sections of your methodology chapter as you complete each stage; for example, once you have undertaken your sampling, you can start writing up your sampling strategy for your methodology chapter.

As noted, an important aspect of all methodology chapters is justifying your decisions. It is worthwhile noting down your justifications at the different stages, by asking yourself:

- Why was that the most appropriate approach or method?
- Why were the alternatives not suitable?
- What factors influenced your decision?

An activity has been created in Box 7.4 to help you consider the justifications for your decision.

Box 7.4   Student Activity 13

Activity 13: Justifying Your Research

Use the table below to help you consider the justifications required. Examples have been provided to help you.

Decision	Justification	Example
Approach		The project took an interpretivist qualitative approach because the research questions called for data that explored subjective experiences.
Method		The most suitable method was semi-structured interviewing because it ensured flexibility in the interview while still ensuring all topics were discussed. Focus groups were considered, but the aim is to understand individual, not collective, experiences.
Sample		Purposive sampling was chosen due to its time and resource effectiveness. The strict criteria for participation meant that a non-probability sample was required.
Data collection (if applicable)		30-minute recorded interviews due to time constraints and ease of transcribing.
Analysis		Inductive thematic analysis to ensure the themes come from the data.

You should also ensure that before writing your methodology chapter you have considered the **literature** on research methods carefully so that your justifications and understanding of research methods can be evidenced. You should have been referring to the literature whilst designing and undertaking your research, so it is a good idea to keep organised notes of what literature you referred to and how that literature strengthens your justifications.

Tips for Writing Your Methodology Chapter

Supervisors get asked many questions when their students are writing their methodology chapter. Below are some of the most frequently asked ones and the advice we give, but always check with your supervisor in case your institution has different guidance.

- Methodology chapters should be written in the past tense – methodology chapters discuss what you *did*
- Personal reflections can be written in first person where appropriate (such as in a reflections section), but the chapter should largely be written in third person
- Set out your structure before you start writing so you know what discussions will be going where
- Additional information such as consent forms, information sheets, interview schedules, and coding frameworks should be referred to in the methodology chapter but placed in your appendices (see Chapter 9)
- Subheadings should be used so that whoever is reading your dissertation can navigate the chapter easily
- Do not include unnecessary detail, such as saying you were late turning up to undertake a focus group because your bus was cancelled
- The aim of the chapter is not to just describe what you did, but to explain how you did it and why you did it
- Remember to acknowledge and discuss problems, obstacles, and limitations of your project. It is not expected to be perfect; all students face difficulties during their dissertation, and it is important you highlight these and whether you were able to overcome them or not

Summary and Checklist

This chapter has outlined the purpose and importance of your methodology chapter. The chapter has explained what content needs to be included, provided suggested structures, and offered guidance on preparing and writing the chapter. Before moving on to the next chapter, complete the checklist in Box 7.5.

Box 7.5 Checklist

1   Understood the importance of a methodology chapter ☐
2   Created a draft structure for your methodology chapter ☐
3   Identified relevant literature to include ☐
4   Completed Activity 13 to justify your decisions ☐

Further Reading

Fox, B.H. and Jennings, W.G. (2014) How to write a methodology and results section for empirical research. *Journal of Criminal Justice Education*, 25(2), pp. 137–156.

Rudestam, K.E. and Newton, R.R. (2015) *Surviving Your Dissertation: A Comprehensive Guide To Content And Process*. London: Sage. Chapter 5.

Chapter 8

Findings and Discussion

Overview

This chapter discusses the process of writing up your findings and discussion in a dissertation. This is often a stage that students find difficult, and the time needed to undertake this stage should not be underestimated. Whatever type of dissertation you have undertaken, you will (hopefully) have found something that helps answer your research question(s). The difficult task is often how to communicate what you have found in an effective manner. By this stage in your dissertation, you will have collected the information you need to answer your research question; this chapter aims to help you organise that information so you can communicate what you have found.

By the end of this chapter you should:

- Understand the importance of your academic voice
- Understand the difference between findings and discussions
- Understand the steps involved in writing up findings and discussions

Developing Your Academic Voice

In any dissertation, it is important that your own voice is demonstrated throughout. This means that anyone reading your dissertation is clear on your position, your arguments, and the conclusions that you make. To develop your academic voice, you need to generate your own arguments. It is not enough to restate the arguments of others; instead, you should bring together the evidence you gathered (whether it is library-based or empirical) and create your own position. This should be evident in all of your chapters; for example, in literature reviews

DOI: 10.4324/9781003016335-9

you need to apply a **critical evaluation** of existing literature (see Chapter 4 of this text), in the methodology chapter you need be **persuasive** regarding the methods employed (see Chapter 7 of this text), and in your discussion of the findings you need to **convince** the reader that your position is supported by the evidence you have collected. When writing up your findings, you ought to be thinking critically about your evidence and reflecting on what the evidence is actually telling you. It is beyond the scope of this text to go into detail on critical thinking and writing (for further guidance, see Cottrell, 2011 and Williams, 2014), but you should understand the importance of critical thinking in your academic studies. In the same way as writing an essay, you need to be creating evidence-based arguments in the discussion of your findings. Using the "So What?" approach is a beneficial way to ensure that your discussions move beyond descriptive accounts of literature to thinking more critically about why you are making particular statements (see Box 8.1).

Box 8.1 Top Tips: The "So What" Approach to Writing

A useful method when writing up your dissertation findings and arguments is to always ask yourself *So what?*

- What is interesting, important, or unique about what you have found?
- What does this tell us that we did not already know?
- What are the implications of what you have found/what you are arguing?

Every time you write an argument or are discussing your findings, take a moment to reflect and consider what it contributes to answering your research question(s).

Using clear phrasing in your writing can help ensure your arguments are transparent, which in turn strengthens your academic voice. You also ought to consider the strength of a statement you want to make; it is important not to make assertions if there is only partial evidence to support them. Academic writing will use **hedgers** and **boosters** depending on the argument it is making. Hedging is applied when you want to demonstrate caution, which is often the case when evidence is conflicted or not robust enough. Boosters are applied when there

Table 8.1 Strengthening Your Academic Voice When Writing Up

Writing Purpose	Example Phrasing
Highlighting limitations of previous work	Previous research on terrorism has **neglected** to...
Discussing theoretical limitations	The theory **fails** to account for...
Showing caution: using hedging	This theory **may** be able to explain...
Showing certainty: using boosters	The evidence **clearly** demonstrates...
Showing the significance of evidence to your project	**Collectively**, the evidence from existing studies supports the position that...
Emphasising a crucial finding	This finding is **important** because...
Relating findings to previous research	These findings **support** the previous research by (author), who also found that...
Showing that findings are distinct from previous research	These findings **call into question** previous studies because...

is certainty in the argument you are making, because the argument is clearly supported by evidence. See Table 8.1 for some examples of phrasing that can help strengthen your academic voice. For further guidance on academic writing in dissertations, please see Greetham (2014) listed in the further reading.

Findings and Discussions in Library-Based Projects

In a library-based dissertation it is probable that your findings (i.e., what you have found from existing literature) will run through more than one chapter. Your dissertation is likely to have an introduction, a short methodology discussion of how you undertook the research, and a review of existing literature, followed by two or more chapters that address your research question(s). It is expected that a library-based project includes:

- A logical structure to answering the research question
- Critical discussions of existing theories and evidence
- An emphasis on the originality/uniqueness of what you have found from the literature
- Conclusions that are valid and consistent with the evidence discussed

Box 8.2 provides some suggested steps to help you start writing up your findings from the existing literature.

Box 8.2 Top Tips: Steps to Writing Up Your Library-Based Project

Step 1: Collect and read the relevant materials (books/journals/policy documents/research reports)

Step 2: Organise what you have found from your reading (according to key themes/topics/evidence)

Step 3: Draw out the key findings from the organised material (using the method you have chosen)

Step 4: Devise chapter structures based on key topics/themes

Step 5: Critically discuss the findings and how they help answer your research question(s)

Organising Your Findings

You need to plan how to structure your arguments after you have gone through the material collected. How you structure these will be very dependent on the type of library-based project you have undertaken. For example, if you have undertaken a historical dissertation, then the timeline may be an important factor in your structure. You may have analysed literature according to types of studies, theoretical frameworks, or key themes, which will influence the order in which you discuss the material in your dissertation.

It is important that, whatever structure you devise, it is logical: that means there is a clear rationale for discussing one aspect of your findings before moving on to the next. For example, Morrison (2013) structured the dissertation according to different time periods to trace changes in the literature, whereas Meyer (2020) organised the findings according to different perspectives on the topic, grouping literature according to the viewpoints. There is no right or wrong way to organise and structure a library-based project, and it is common for the structure to be amended as writing progresses. However, you ought to create a draft structure to help with writing, and ensuring you have organised your data accordingly will help you achieve this.

Discussing Your Findings

One of the most difficult aspects of a library-based dissertation is to avoid it being overly descriptive. Your task is not to describe what we already know; your task is to use what we already know and **apply it** to answer your research question(s). The important thing to remember in a library-based project is to treat the information you have collected as **data**. You have sampled a range of literature to answer your research question, and the next stage is to critically analyse the literature to answer it. In doing so, you ought to be scrutinising existing sources to examine how valid the arguments presented are. This could be in the methods they employ to collect and analyse data, the sampling strategy used, the theoretical framework they have applied, and/or the conclusions that they have come to. You should also note down where existing literature supports or opposes other literature, and how you can infer conclusions for any opposing evidence.

When you are discussing what the existing literature demonstrates, you need to consider how that information helps you answer your research question(s). How does what you have found compare to previous research, and how are you filling the gap in knowledge that you identified from your literature review? Reminding your reader of the objectives of the research, and how your discussions help meet those objectives, demonstrates the focus and **cohesiveness** of your dissertation. Each chapter in a library-based dissertation must have a purpose and fit with the mission of the dissertation as a whole. Including an introduction and conclusion to each of your chapters gives you an opportunity to clearly state the purpose of each of the chapters and how they contribute to the objectives of the dissertation. Box 8.3 offers some tips to ensuring your findings and discussion meet the academic standard expected.

Box 8.3 Top Tips: Dos and Don'ts in Library-Based Projects

1   Don't just summarise what other authors have written. Do use their evidence to develop your own arguments.
2   Don't make claims that are unsubstantiated with evidence. Do cite more than one piece of evidence to support core arguments.

3   Don't assume that all published research is valid and reliable. Do use your knowledge of research methods to scrutinise existing work.

4   Don't create chapters that read like annotated bibliographies. Do group existing literature together that relates to the argument(s) you are putting forward.

Findings and Discussions in Empirical Projects

In an empirical project, your findings will most likely be positioned after your methodology chapter. The methodology chapter discusses how you collected and analysed your data, and your findings discuss what you have found from the data. There is no strict rule on how to present your findings and discussion in a dissertation. Supervisors will often get asked questions such as "Do I need to write a separate findings and discussion chapter?" "How many findings chapters do I need? ""How much of my data do I put in my findings? "These are all common questions, and the most straightforward answer is: **it depends on your project**.

It is important to note the **distinction between findings and discussion**. The findings section is what you found from your research; for example, your survey results, or the key themes from your interviews, or the contents of your media analysis. The discussion section considers what those findings mean, what they are telling us, and how they contribute to existing literature in the field. In some dissertations the findings and discussion each have their own distinct chapter, while in other dissertations the findings are presented along with a discussion of what they mean. The type of data you have, and your preference for writing it up, will determine what structure you opt for. It is always advisable to discuss these options with your supervisor prior to writing up.

Whatever way you decide to present this part of your dissertation, it is expected that all empirical projects will include:

- A presentation of what the main findings of the analysis are
- A discussion of the findings
- A discussion of the relationship of the findings to existing literature
- An emphasis on the originality/uniqueness of what you have found from the data
- Conclusions that are valid and consistent with the data collected

Box 8.4 provides some suggested steps to help you start writing up your findings from your research.

Box 8.4 Top Tips: Steps to Writing Up Your Empirical Project

Step 1: Organise what you have found from your data after analysis
(according to key themes/topics/evidence)
Step 2: Draw out the key findings from the organised material that help answer your research question
Step 3: Identify what existing literature (from your literature review) your findings support/oppose
Step 4: Critically discuss the findings and how they help answer your research question(s)

Quantitative Findings

The findings, or results, section of your dissertation is where you report on the key findings of your research. It is common in quantitative research for the results to be in a separate chapter from the discussion. For example, Heap (2008) undertook secondary data analysis of the British Crime Survey (now known as the Crime Survey for England and Wales) and presented all her main findings in one chapter. The chapter contained the relevant graphs and tables and interpreted what these were highlighting. Heap's findings chapter was followed by a discussion chapter that considered in depth what those findings meant. Similarly, Toomey (2019) separated her findings from the survey she undertook, interpreted the findings in one chapter and followed it with a chapter containing an in-depth discussion of what those findings meant. Price (2011), on the other hand, presented the findings of her questionnaire and included the discussion alongside the findings rather than separating them out. Thus, you can decide whether to present and discuss in the same chapter or split the findings and the discussion into distinct chapters.

When you present your quantitative findings and analysis, it is important that you interpret what these findings mean; avoid leaving your reader guessing why you have included them. Other important points to note when writing up your findings are:

- You should deploy your data selectively to illustrate the most relevant material
- You should only include graphs, figures and/or tables when they are needed to help visualise the data
- You should label your data with a title and number
- The findings should be orientated to your research question(s)
- You should present any statistical testing in the appropriate format

Qualitative Findings

In qualitative research, you need to present your findings by choosing extracts of the data that support the arguments you are making. These extracts could be from interview/focus group transcripts, images, or extracts from media or policy documents. Just like quantitative data, you need to interpret the findings by referring to the extracts somewhere in your text. A reader should know why you have chosen those particular extracts to include in your findings.

Unlike statistical testing that has a specific format for presenting, there are no rules for presenting qualitative research. However, all qualitative data presented ought to be labelled, and the labelling needs to be explained (this normally occurs in the introductory paragraph of the chapter). For example, you can give participants a simple label such as a letter or number, or you could give them pseudonyms; the complexity of the label you give your extracts will depend on your sample. See Table 8.2 for some examples of how you can label qualitative data extracts.

You can choose whether to separate your findings chapter(s) from your discussion chapter, as Newbold (2011) did in her dissertation, or combine the findings with the discussion, like in De Camargo's (2012) dissertation. Either way, you have to decide which extracts of data will be the most beneficial for evidencing the arguments you are making. Other important points to note when writing up your findings are:

- You should deploy your data selectively to illustrate the most relevant material
- The findings should be orientated to your research question(s)
- Your findings should be organised logically

You should ensure your arguments are supported by more than one data extract; avoid making grand claims based on only one person's experience/opinion.

Table 8.2 Examples of Labelling Qualitative Data

Example Data	Example Label Explanation	Example Labels
Ten participants: five female, three male, two undisclosed	Each participant given a corresponding letter + number F = Female M = Male U = Undisclosed	F(1) M(3) U(2)
Seven interview participants, all female	Each participant given a pseudonym to protect identity	Sarah Bethan Laura
20 newspaper articles from three different tabloids	Each article given a corresponding letter + number Daily Mail = DM The Sun = TS Daily Express = DE	DM1 TS2 DE3
Two focus groups, each with six participants	Each participant given a number and corresponding focus group Focus Group A = FGA Focus Group B = FGB	FGA (1) FGB (2)

Discussing Qualitative and Quantitative Data

Your discussion of the findings, whether included with or separated from your findings chapter, is one of the most important parts of your empirical dissertation. The discussion is where you are able to situate your research findings against previous research and provide an in-depth discussion about what your findings mean for the field of study. In the discussion you are required to discuss your findings in the context of existing theory and research. To do this, you need to relate your findings back to your literature review, and you can bring in additional literature if required. To contextualise your findings, consider doing the following:

- Utilising existing theory to make sense of your findings
- Comparing your research findings with previous studies
- Demonstrating how you have filled the research gap you highlighted in your introductory chapters
- Discussing how your research will contribute to knowledge/practice in the field

The discussion should be written using the *So What?* approach outlined at the start of this chapter. Reflect on what you have found, why it is relevant, and what the implications of the findings are. You can also use the discussion to highlight any limitations of your data, such as validity and reliability. Have a look at the examples in Box 8.5 of where findings are related back to existing literature; these are all taken from published dissertations. In each of the examples, the students contextualise their research with existing studies by discussing similarities and differences in findings.

Box 8.5 Examples of Contextualising Findings

Example 1: Harrop (2019: 29–30)

These findings firstly support the view of Citron and Franks (2014), who hold that sexual privacy is a fundamental right in order to protect sexual autonomy, and secondly, McGlynn and Rackley (2016), who have long argued for RP [revenge porn] to be recognised as a form of abuse. Despite participants' views leaning towards support for RP criminalisation, only (n=4) participants were able to confidently say if RP was currently a criminal offence in the UK. Although awareness has been raised via government strategies (Ministry of Justice, 2015), this finding could indicate a need for more attention in this area.

Example 2: Williams (2017: 30)

Current findings provide further support for those attained in from previous studies (Morgan et al., 2009; Nutt et al., 2007; Nutt et al., 2010). In the study conducted by Morgan et al. (2009), findings revealed a high correlation between drug experts' and drug users' opinions on the harms of various illicit substances, but no such relationship between harm and drug classification. The current study adds to this, by finding for no such correlation existing in a student population.

Example 3: Cecilia (2019: 26)

This study attempted to verify Chiotti's (2009) and Landor's (2009) hypotheses on media's representation of FSOs [female sex offenders]. Hence, it could be confirmed that media depict unusual women in a way that tries to excuse them (Chiotti,

2009). Having found no – or very little – references to words such as "paedophile", "paedophilia", "rapist", "offender" and "crazy", this study confirms that Italian media might not want to label FSOs the same way they usually do with males. Apparently, abusive Italian women are neither paedophiles nor rapists; they are not offenders nor mad criminals.

Planning Your Findings and Discussion Chapters

Writing your findings and discussion can seem daunting at first. You have gathered and analysed a lot of information, and it may be overwhelming trying to organise everything. Your task, no matter what type of dissertation you have undertaken, is to ensure your arguments are clear, relevant, logical, and contextualised. It is therefore worth taking time to plan out how you will write your findings and discussion. Things you should consider when planning are:

- How will you structure your findings?
- Will your findings and discussions be integrated or separated?
- Which findings are most relevant for answering your research question(s)?
- What literature can be best applied to contextualise your findings?

To help you start thinking about some of these questions, please complete the activity in Box 8.6. Please also remember that it is likely you will write various drafts of your findings and discussion until you are happy with the structure and content. It is very common for these chapters to be reworked after the initial drafts have been produced and, as always, if you are struggling you should seek support from your supervisor.

Box 8.6 Student Activity 14

Activity 14: Planning Your Findings and Discussions

Try following these suggested steps to help you plan your findings and discussions write-up.

1   Write down your research question(s) somewhere so you keep focussed on what you are aiming to achieve with your findings

2   Write down your main findings from your research and reflect on which findings are addressing the research question(s)

3   Consider how you want to organise your findings – this might be thematically, chronologically, or according to specific research questions

4   Return to your literature review and map which theories/ studies relate to each of your main findings; also note down areas of literature you need to read more on

5   After you have mapped the relevant literature, note down beside each study whether your findings support, oppose, or add to existing knowledge

6   Start writing out your findings and decide whether it makes sense to discuss each finding individually, or present all the findings and create a separate discussion in a distinct chapter

Summary and Checklist

This chapter has provided guidance on writing up your findings and discussions. This is an exciting part of the research process, as it is at this stage you can put your own stamp on your research topic. This stage enables you to put forward your evidence-based arguments and contribute to academic knowledge. Ensuring you carefully plan and structure your findings and discussions, and develop your academic voice, will all result in a robust dissertation of academic quality. Please complete the checklist in Box 8.7 before moving on to the final chapter of this text.

Box 8.7 Checklist

1   Read one of the suggested readings to understand how to create your own arguments   ☐

2   Discussed with your supervisor the best way to structure your findings and discussions   ☐

3   Completed Activity 14 from this chapter   ☐

4	Checked that every argument you make is supported with robust evidence from either existing literature or your own data ☐
5	Checked that you have fully answered your research question(s) and have communicated this clearly in your discussions ☐

Further Reading

Greetham, B. (2014) *How to Write Your Undergraduate Dissertation*. 2nd edn. Basingstoke: Palgrave. Parts 7 and 8.

Rudestam, K.E. and Newton, R.R. (2015) *Surviving Your Dissertation: A Comprehensive Guide To Content And Process*. London: Sage. Chapters 6 and 7.

Walliman, N.S.R. (2014) *Your Undergraduate Dissertation: The Essential Guide for Success*. 2nd Edition. London: Sage. Chapter 15.

Chapter 9

Writing Up and Presenting Your Dissertation

Overview

This chapter discusses how to write up your dissertation, ensuring it has effective introductions and conclusions and a logical structure, and is coherent throughout. It will also cover the additional content you find in dissertations, including abstracts and appendices. The chapter aims to assist you in ensuring your dissertation is presented to the academic standards required.

By the end of this chapter you should:

- Be able to structure your dissertation effectively
- Be able to write an abstract, introduction and conclusion
- Understand what to look for when proofreading your work

Writing-Up Process

Writing up refers to the process of bringing all the work you have done on your dissertation together in a coherent way. You need to be able to pull together the existing literature, your findings, and your answer to the research question(s) so that the whole project has a clear focus from start to finish. Writing up can be very time-consuming, so it is important not to underestimate how much time is required to complete this process.

Punch (2014: 341) describes a dissertation as a "series of decisions", and your job in writing up the dissertation is to make it clear how and why you made those decisions. Your decisions will relate to how you devised your research question, why you chose particular methods, how you analysed the data you collected, and how you came to your conclusions. A successful dissertation is one that has a clear path of

DOI: 10.4324/9781003016335-10

decision-making from the start to the end, with justifications offered at each stage.

Box 9.1 offers three groups of top tips for writing up which will help you ensure clarity, fluidity and consistency. A dissertation should be very clear from the outset in what it is aiming to achieve and why, and it should be clear what was achieved and how it was achieved. **Clarity** gives your reader confidence that you have obvious focus and know how to achieve the aims of the research question(s). **Fluidity** ensures that your dissertation is easy to follow and has a clear structure throughout. Signposting, as you would in an essay, helps your reader to know where you are going next in the dissertation and how each chapter follows on from the previous one. The final group of tips relate to **consistency**, which certifies that every part of your dissertation is directly related to your research question(s). If your dissertation loses focus or goes off track in places, this can make it difficult to follow and it can appear as though you have lost your train of thought. Make sure that you start your dissertation with core aims and ensure you have met these by the time you write your conclusion.

Box 9.1 Top Tips for Writing Up

Tip 1: Clarity	Tip 2: Fluidity	Tip 3: Consistency
Ensure these are clearly articulated in your dissertation: • What was carried out? • Why it was carried out? • How it was carried out? • What was found? • What do those findings mean?	Ensure there are clear links between each of your chapters. • End one chapter by signposting the next chapter • Start each chapter as a continuation of the previous one	Ensure you remain consistent throughout. • The aims and objectives set out in the beginning should be achieved by the end • You should answer your research question and come to a conclusion • Every chapter should be focused on answering the research question

Writing Your Introductory Chapter

The introductory chapter will most likely be the last chapter you write in your dissertation, because you cannot introduce your dissertation until you have completed it. The introduction is the first chapter your reader will read, so it must make a good impression and grab their attention.

The introduction needs to set out very clearly what the topic for investigation is and what the dissertation is aiming to achieve. Your research question should be articulated clearly from the start. Your introduction should:

• Define what the topic is
• Explain why the topic is important and worth researching
• Contextualise the topic in the broader field and describe what are you adding to existing knowledge
• Outline your main research question(s)
• Define any key concepts used throughout the dissertation
• Introduce what each chapter of the dissertation covers

You can use subheadings in introductory chapters which clearly present each part of the introductory chapter; for examples, see Nash (2019), Shearman (2021), and Spiller (2021). In all three of these examples, it is clear what the authors are researching, why they are researching the topic, and what they aim to achieve. You should also consider the key concepts that will be applied in your dissertation; for example, if your topic is on young people, what age group are you defining as "young" and why? If your topic is on gangs, then again you will need to explain how you are defining a gang, as this concept is debated frequently in the literature. Always remember to provide academic, rather than dictionary, definitions for key terms and concepts.

Complete the activity in Box 9.2 to help you write your introductory chapter. Once you have the key points noted from the activity, you can start discussing each of them in more depth to write your chapter. The most important thing to remember is to **grab your readers' attention**, drawing them in to your study by explaining the originality and why the study is important.

Box 9.2 Student Activity 15

Activity 15: Planning Your Introductory Chapter

Write out a paragraph answering each of the following questions:

- What is your topic?
- Why is your topic important to research?
- What are you trying to achieve?
- Where does your research fit in to the broader subject field?
- What should a reader expect from your dissertation; how is it structured?

Writing Your Concluding Chapter

The conclusion is the last chapter your reader will look at, so it should make a good lasting impression. It should pull the whole dissertation together and bring it to a close. The conclusion should mirror the introduction by restating the aims and objectives, and it should answer the research question(s) you set out with. It is also a chance to reflect on the dissertation as a whole, by considering what you found (or did not find), what went well (and not well), and what you would recommend for future research. Your concluding chapter should:

- Restate the aims and objectives of the study
- Reflect on how you answered your research question (what you did and why, and whether there were any limitations)
- Discuss the overall findings (Did you answer your questions? What are the implications and relevance of what you have found?)
- Offer recommendations for further research or policy or professional practice on your topic (if applicable)

The conclusion should not just be a summary of what you wrote in each chapter; you need to consider the overall contribution of what you have undertaken, its achievements and its limitations. Some dissertation projects may not come to a firm answer to the research question, and that is okay; in many cases a dissertation can raise more questions. If you can identify what data we need more of on a topic, and what direction future research should take, then you are still making a contribution. These are what we refer to as **recommendations**. It is also important to be honest in your concluding chapter: avoid making grand statements or conclusions if your data does not support them or is not robust enough to support them. As stated previously in this text, your dissertation will most likely have some limitations, and that is to be expected. Showing your awareness of these demonstrates your research knowledge. Complete the activity in Box 9.3 to help you plan out your concluding chapter. Once you have noted down the key points, you can start to write your conclusion more fully.

Box 9.3 Student Activity 16

Activity 16: Planning Your Concluding Chapter

Write out a paragraph answering each of the following questions:

- What did you aim to achieve with your dissertation and why?
- Did you achieve your objectives and answer your research question(s)?
- What key contributions does your dissertation make to the subject area/policy/practice?
- What were the limitations to your dissertation?
- Would you have done anything differently?
- What further research needs to be undertaken on the topic?

Structuring Your Dissertation

Chapter 1 highlighted that there are different ways to structure your dissertation, and how you do it will be dependent on the type of dissertation you have undertaken and the contents of each of your chapters. Please refer to Tables 1.2 and 1.3 in Chapter 1 for example structures that your dissertation may follow. This section will provide an overview of the different sections that you may be required to include in a dissertation in addition to your main chapters. These include:

- Abstract
- Acknowledgements
- List of acronyms
- Contents page
- Appendices

Abstracts

One of the most common questions supervisors get asked by students is "What is an abstract?" An abstract is simply a summary of a piece of research; in this case, a summary of your dissertation. You will notice that all journal articles usually have an abstract at the beginning summarising what the research paper contains. The abstract allows readers to get a sense of what your project is about, and what your research found and concluded, without having to read the whole piece of work. Abstracts are short, normally around 200–300 words (it is recommended you check with your institution what length of abstract is expected), and should come at the beginning of your dissertation.

An abstract is normally one or two paragraphs that summarise the key points of your dissertation. In the abstract you should include:

- What your dissertation topic is
- A brief context to your topic
- A summary of your methodological approach
- A summary of your key findings
- Overall conclusion

An example has been provided in Box 9.4 and it has been colour coded so you can see the different sections that ought to be included. Have a go at the activity in Box 9.5 to help you write your abstract.

Box 9.4 Example Dissertation Abstract*

This dissertation explores whether there are any differences in the narrative reporting of burglary in local and national newspapers.	**Topic**
News outlets are criticised for their misrepresentations of crime, offenders and victims, regularly overrepresenting violent crime and crimes committed by people from socially disadvantaged backgrounds. The way in which a news story is told can be just as powerful as what is covered, thus understanding what narrative is used helps to explore news coverage in more depth.	**Context**
In order to explore if any differences lie between the geographical news reporting, this dissertation undertook a narrative analysis of 30 news stories across a four-month period.	**Method**
The research found that local newspapers used more emotive and punitive language than national newspapers. It also found more sympathetic language used to describe victims of burglary.	**Findings**
The dissertation concludes that further research is required to understand whether these different styles of reporting have any impact over the readers' views towards crime and punishment.	**Conclusion**

*Paragraph spacing has been added to visually represent the different components. This is not necessary when you write your own abstract.

Box 9.5 Student Activity 17

Activity 17: Writing Your Abstract

Try to summarise each of your chapters in just one or two sentences using the questions below, then put these sentences together to create an abstract.

Topic – What is your dissertation topic?

Why is your topic important? What are you trying to find out?

What methods did you use to answer you research question(s)?

Findings – What did you find out? Did the findings support/challenge existing research?

What can you conclude from your dissertation? Any recommendations?

Acknowledgements

It is common for students to include an acknowledgements section in their dissertation to recognise and thank those that helped them complete their dissertation. This is usually an optional section, and it is entirely a personal choice what to include. If you are considering an acknowledgements section but unsure what to include, have a look at the suggestions below:

- Thanking your supervisor
- Thanking friends and/or family
- Thanking research participants
- Thanking organisations (such as those who granted you access)
- Thanking academic/support/professional services staff

Your acknowledgements can be as long or as short as you like and can be written in first person. If you do include an acknowledgements section, it should come at the start of your dissertation (normally before or after your abstract). Check with your supervisor if you are unsure where to place it.

List of Acronyms

If your dissertation includes a lot of acronyms (abbreviations), then you can include a list of these at the start of your dissertation, normally after your introductory chapter. This can be beneficial for anyone reading your dissertation, as they can refer to your list if there are any acronyms they want to clarify while reading your work. It is not necessary to include this list if you have only used one or two acronyms in your dissertation, but if you have several then it is worth creating a list.

Table of Contents

It is routine for students to include a contents page for their dissertation, just as you would find a contents page in a textbook. A contents page lists each chapter of your dissertation and informs the reader what page each section and chapter is on. A table of contents can either be created using just the chapter headings or also include page numbers for the subheadings in each chapter (see the examples in Box 9.6). There are many helpful guides and videos available online that walk you through how to create a contents page using different word processing software; it is also recommended you speak to your university for any help guides they can provide.

Box 9.6 Example Contents Pages

Example Contents Pages

First Level Heading Only		First and Sub-Level Headings	
Abstract	1	Abstract	1
Acknowledgements	2	Acknowledgements	2
Introduction	3	Introduction	3
Literature review	7	Research rationale	4
Methodology	15	Aims of study	5
Discussion of Findings	23	Layout of dissertation	6

First Level Heading Only		First and Sub-Level Headings	
Conclusion	35	Literature Review	7
Bibliography	38	Sub-heading 1	7
Appendices	42	Sub-heading 2	10
		Sub-heading 3	13
		Methodology	15
		Approach	15
		Method	15
		Sample	16
		Data collection	16
		Analysis	19
		Ethics	21
		Discussion of Findings	23
		Sub-heading 1	23
		Sub-heading 2	27
		Sub-heading 3	31
		Conclusion	35
		Bibliography	38
		Appendices	42
		A: Interview schedule	42
		B: Consent form	43
		C: Information sheet	44
		D: Coding framework	45

Appendices

An appendix is a section at the end of your dissertation where you can include accompanying information that you refer to in other parts of your dissertation. Each item in an appendix should have its own title and letter or number (e.g., Appendix 1 or Appendix A). Appendices are used for supplementary material that you want your reader to see but does not belong in the main body of your dissertation. Not all dissertations will require an appendix, so speak to your supervisor if you are unsure whether you need one or not. The type of information that can be found in appendices includes, but is not limited to:

• Supplementary figures and tables
• Survey/interview/focus group questions
• Blank consent forms
• Participant information sheets
• Recruitment posters/adverts

- Coding matrixes
- Letters/email correspondences
- Ethics forms

Presenting Your Dissertation

It is vitally important your dissertation is presented correctly before you submit. Some institutions will include presentation in the grading of your work, so you want to ensure you do not lose marks because of poor presentation. Presentation routinely includes the following:

- Punctuation, grammar, and spelling
- Appropriate use of paragraphs
- Correct presentation of quotes
- Correct referencing using the appropriate style
- Good overall presentation of work

Your institution will offer guidance on how your dissertation should be presented, and it is important you take time to read these requirements. They may require you to use a certain referencing style, font, and layout, and you should follow this. There are some common errors supervisors see in the presentation of dissertations that are normally a result of poor proofreading. It is recommended that you (or someone you know) thoroughly proofread your work prior to submitting, to correct any presentation issues. A helpful tip is to read through your whole dissertation twice. Read it through the first time to detect any issues in the clarity, fluidity and consistency of your writing. Then read it through the second time to identify any presentational errors. You will likely have read each chapter fully, but it is imperative you read the dissertation as a whole to make certain the structure, the arguments, and the presentation are consistent throughout. Box 9.7 offers some top tips for proofreading your work to help you. You can use the activity in Box 9.8 to ensure you are presenting a piece of work that meets academic standards.

Box 9.7 Top Tips: Proofreading

1   If possible, print off your dissertation; it is easier to spot errors on a paper copy than an electronic copy
2   Check for any inconsistencies in font style, font size and spacing

3   Ensure you do not have page-long paragraphs or paragraphs of only one or two lines
4   Ensure none of your text is out of line with the page
5   Ensure tables, graphs and figures are not split between pages
6   Check that all chapters start on a new page
7   Double check all your references are correctly presented, and everything cited in the text is listed in your bibliography/reference list
8   Check for spelling/grammar issues. Do not rely on your word processing software as this can lead to errors
9   Dedicate time to proofreading, and avoid trying to proofread the whole dissertation at one time

Box 9.8 Student Activity 18

Activity 18: Presenting Your Work Checklist

Use this checklist to help you when reviewing your work

Check	✓
Do all your pages have page numbers?	
Is your reference list formatted according to your institution's requirements?	
Are all your citations in your reference list (and vice versa)?	
Are all your chapters numbered with headings?	
Have you ensured your paragraphs are an appropriate length?	
Have you started all chapters on a new page?	
Have you used a suitable font?	

Have you used a suitable font size?	
Have you used appropriate line spacing?	
Have you included a list of abbreviations (if applicable)?	
Have you included a table of contents?	
Do all your main chapters have a short introduction and summary?	
Have you included all supplementary information in appendices?	
Have you included an abstract (if required)?	

Summary and Checklist

This chapter has offered guidance on writing and presenting your dissertation. Please see the suggested further reading to help you with this process, and complete the checklist in Box 9.9 to help you keep track when writing up. Once you have completed the write-up, you have finished your dissertation. At this point you should **celebrate your achievement** and be proud of the piece of work you submit.

Box 9.9 Checklist

1 You have read your institution's guidance on structuring and presenting your work ☐
2 You have discussed with your supervisor what sections need to be included ☐
3 You have completed Activities 15–18 of this chapter ☐

4 You have ensured each of your main chapters has a
  short introduction and summary with signposting ☐
5 You have set aside time for your work to be proofread ☐
6 You have created a bibliography/reference list
  according to your institution's referencing style ☐

Further Reading

Burnett, J. (2009) *Doing Your Social Science Dissertation.* London: Sage. Chapter 11.

Caufield, L. and Hill, J. (2018) *Criminological Skills and Research for Beginners.* 2nd edn. London: Routledge. Chapter 18.

References

Brown, J. (1996) Police research: some critical issues. In: Leishman, F., Loveday, B. and Savage, S.P. (eds.) *Core Issues in Policing*. London: Longman Group Ltd.

Brown, M. (2017) Visual criminology. In: *Oxford Research Encyclopedia of Criminology, April*. Available at: https://doi.org/10.1093/acrefore/978019 0264079.013.206 [Accessed 18 December 2021].

Bryman, A. (2016) *Social Research Methods* 5th edn. Oxford: Oxford University Press.

Burnett, J. (2009) *Doing Your Social Science Dissertation*. London: Sage.

Butters, S. (2021) Perceptions of the use and effectiveness of victim personal statements within West Yorkshire Police. *Internet Journal of Criminology*. Available at: https://958be75a-da42-4a45-aafa-549955018b18.filesusr. com/ugd/9280ee_3536c15c6f5a447bafd7f6a89959664a.pdf [Accessed February 2021].

Cashman, H. (2019) To what extent is sexual assault occurring in the night time economy normalised? *Internet Journal of Criminology*. Available at: https://958be75a-da42-4a45-aafa-549955018b18.filesusr.com/ugd/b93dd4_80732622069c4c4fa5f84ddb3721bc06.pdf [Accessed May 2021].

Cashmore, J. (2017) Have community protection officers (CPOs) met expectations? managerial opinions of Nottingham City Council's wardens as policing partners. *Internet Journal of Criminology*. Available at: https://958be75a-da42-4a45-aafa-549955018b18.filesusr.com/ugd/b93dd4_11c303282a9e4ad5b7011276555f3bd8.pdf [Accessed March 2021].

Caufield, L. and Hill, J. (2018) *Criminological Skills and Research for Beginners*, 2nd edn. London: Routledge.

Cecilia, C. (2019) Italian media's representation of female sex offenders 2008–2014: an analysis. *Internet Journal of Criminology*. Available at: https://958be 75a-da42-4a45-aafa-549955018b18.filesusr.com/ugd/b93dd4_06d2315e2 9dd4d4cacb680f7f809ad21.pdf [Accessed May 2021].

Chamberlain, C. (2019) "...It's definitely lost its meaning and what it's for...": the changing motives of LGBT pride and its impact on hate crime against members of LGBT community. *Internet Journal of Criminology*.

Available at: https://958be75a-da42-4a45-aafa-549955018b18.filesusr. com/ugd/b93dd4_7fcaccb5c2a54235a541c98c904a48fd.pdf [Accessed June 2021].

Chiotti, J.M. (2009). *The "Illusive" Female Sex Offender: A Quantitative Content Analysis Of Media Exposure.* PhD Dissertation. Washington State University, USA.

Citron, D. and Franks, M., (2014) Criminalizing Revenge Porn. *Wake Forrest Law Review*, 49. pp. 345–391.

Cottrell, S. (2011) *Critical Thinking Skills: Developing Effective Analysis and Argument* 2nd edn. *Palgrave Study Skills.* Basingstoke: Palgrave.

Cox, P. Shore, H. and Godfrey, B. (2018) 'Using Historical Artefacts, Records and Resources in Criminological Research' in Davies, P. and Francis, P. (Eds.) *Doing Criminological Research* 3rd edn. London: Sage. pp. 179–198.

De Camargo, C. (2012) The Police Uniform: Power, Authority and Culture. *Internet Journal of Criminology.* Available at: https://958be75a-da42-4a45-aafa-549955018b18.filesusr.com/ugd/b93dd4_ba3f7c1b10aa48c9b0cca 98d3239c490.pdf [Accessed July 2021].

Deakin, J. (2011) Sensitive Survey Research: An Oxymoron? In: Davies, P., Francis, P. and Jupp, V. (Eds) *Doing Criminological Research* 2nd edn. pp. 139–160.

Debo-Aina, O. (2021) Silencing the story of the streets: an investigation into how the media and political (mis)representations of UK drill music affects the lives and identities of Black youth in south London. *Leeds Student Law and Criminal Justice Review* 1: 136–165.

Delaney, T. (2013) The EU Plan of Action on Combating Terrorism: an ambiguous and redundant tool of governance. *Internet Journal of Criminology.* Available at: https://958be75a-da42-4a45-aafa-549955018b18.filesusr. com/ugd/b93dd4_26d23f95757b4e07817511c1cd5e8089.pdf [Accessed May 2021].

Duke, K. (2002) Getting beyond the "official line": reflections on dilemmas of access, knowledge and power in researching policy networks. *Journal of Social Policy*, 31(1): 39–59.

Etikan, I., Musa, S. and Alkassim, R., (2015) Comparison of convenience sampling and purposive sampling. *American Journal of Theoretical and Applied Statistics*, 5(1), pp. 1–4.

Fox, B.H. and Jennings, W.G. (2014) How to write a methodology and results section for empirical research. *Journal of Criminal Justice Education*, 25(2): 137–156.

Greetham, B. (2014) *How to Write Your Undergraduate Dissertation* 2nd edn. Basingstoke: Palgrave.

Guillemin, M. and Gillam, L. (2004) Ethics, reflexivity, and "ethically important moments" in research. *Qualitative Inquiry* 10(2), 261.

Harrop, A.R. (2019) "It makes it sound public; it makes it sound seedy and like the images have been created for a mass audience": an explorative study of student perceptions of revenge porn terminology. *Internet Journal of Criminology*. Available at: https://958be75a-da42-4a45-aafa-549955018 b18.filesusr.com/ugd/b93dd4_ac60500d4644498eb7a4168d1f39eb70.pdf [Accessed March 2021].

Heap, V. (2008) Criminal victimisation of the elderly: have rates of crime against the elderly changed relative to overall crime rates? *Internet Journal of Criminology*. Available at: https://958be75a-da42-4a45-aafa-549955018 b18.filesusr.com/ugd/b93dd4_25ad4ded381343b1a51ab70640e4d924.pdf [Accessed March 2021].

Heslop, J. (2019) Drug trafficking, the pressures of transnational organised crime on The National Crime Agency (NCA) and Drug Enforcement Administration (DEA), a comparative analysis of policing strategies within the war against drugs. *Internet Journal of Criminology*. Available at: https:// 958be75a-da42-4a45-aafa-549955018b18.filesusr.com/ugd/b93dd4_ 609060b879bd4caf9fd920f860357ccc.pdf [Accessed February 2021].

Jacklin, A. (2020) Is breaking the law a climate necessity? A qualitative study on the experiences of extinction rebellion members arrested for protesting. *Internet Journal of Criminology*. Available at: https://958be75a-da42-4a45-aafa-549955018b18.filesusr.com/ugd/b93dd4_131fe53bb2884fca883d4 f42e4fd4027.pdf [Accessed April 2021].

Jensen, E.A. and Laurie, C. (2016) *Doing Real Research*. London: Sage.

Killam, L. (2013). *Research terminology simplified: Paradigms, axiology, ontology, epistemology and methodology*. Sudbury, ON: Author.

King, R.D. and Liebling, A. (2007) Doing research in prisons. In: King, R. and Wincup, E. (Eds) *Doing Research on Crime and Justice* 2nd edn. Oxford: Oxford University Press. pp. 431–451.

Landor, R.V. (2009). Double standards? Representation of male vs. female sex offenders in the Australian media. *Griffith Working Papers in Pragmatics and Intercultural Communications*, 2(2), pp. 84–93.

Lee, R.M. (1993) *Doing Research on Sensitive Topics*. London: Sage.

Liebling, A. (1999) Doing Research in Prison: Breaking the Silence? *Theoretical Criminology* 3(2):147–73.

Loiselle, C., Profetto-McGrath, J., Polit, D. and Beck, C. (2010) *Canadian Essentials in Nursing Research,* 3rd edn. United States, Philadelphia: Williams and Wilkins Publishing.

Malmqvist, J., Hellberg, K., Möllas, G., Rose, R. and Shevlin, M. (2019) Conducting the pilot study: a neglected part of the research process? Methodological findings supporting the importance of piloting in qualitative research studies. *International Journal of Qualitative Methods* 18, pp. 1–11.

Martin, C. (2000) Doing Research in a Prison Setting. In: Jupp, V., Davies, P. and Francis, P. (Eds.) *Doing Criminological Research*. London: Sage: pp.217–234.

Matthews, B. and Ross, L. (2010) *Research Methods: A Practical Guide for the Social Sciences*. Essex: Pearson.

McDonnell, M. (2020) "I hope Boris Johnson watches Top Boy": a synthetic and critical analysis of popular culture. *Internet Journal of Criminology*.

Available at: https://958be75a-da42-4a45-aafa-549955018b18.filesusr. com/ugd/b93dd4_1807ddfd8b43452ea26eb09966c916d8.pdf [Accessed May 2021].

McGlynn, C. and Rackley, E. (2016) Image-Based Sexual Abuse: More Than Just "Revenge Porn". Available at: www.birmingham.ac.uk/Documents/ collegeartslaw/law/research/bham-law-spotlight-IBSA.pdf [Accessed 21 July 2019].

Meyer, G. (2020) The criminalisation of abortion in America: Waging war on women's rights. A genealogy. *Internet Journal of Criminology*. Available at: https://958be75a-da42-4a45-aafa-549955018b18.filesusr.com/ugd/ b93dd4_5bc7cba9aec74b5295d5ebbbb26db010.pdf [Accessed June 2021].

Ministry of Justice (2015) Revenge Porn: Be Aware B4 You Share. Available at: www.gov.uk/government/publications/revenge-porn-be-aware-b4-youshare [Accessed 3 September 2019].

Moore, S. (2014) *Crime and the Media*. Basingstoke: Palgrave.

Morgan, C. J., Muetzelfeldt, L., Muetzelfeldt, M., Nutt, D. J. and Curran, H. V. (2009). Harms associated with psychoactive substances: Findings of the UK national drug survey. *Journal of Psychopharmacology*, 24(2), pp. 147–153.

Morrison, G. (2013) I shop therefore I am; does the society of consumption drive criminal activity in late liquid modernity? *Internet Journal of Criminology*. Available at: https://958be75a-da42-4a45-aafa-549955018 b18.filesusr.com/ugd/b93dd4_e5a687198e474559bb68d674eb1bfd4b.pdf [Accessed April 2021].

Nash, S. (2019) Joint enterprise, BAME groups and gang narratives. *Internet Journal of Criminology*. Available at: https://958be75a-da42-4a45-aafa-549955018b18.filesusr.com/ugd/b93dd4_1bddaf5be2b84670ab5686f05 6a850e9.pdf [Accessed May 2021].

Newbold, K. (2011) An evaluation of the offender assessment system as an assessment tool for the National Probation Service. *Internet Journal of Criminology*. Available at: https://958be75a-da42-4a45-aafa-549955018 b18.filesusr.com/ugd/b93dd4_b7cf661327cd46eb8684068847c3b5d6.pdf [Accessed June 2021].

Noaks L. and Wincup, E. (2004) *Criminological Research: Understanding Qualitative Methods*. London: Sage.

Nutt, D., King, L.A., Saulsbury, W. and Blakemore, C. (2007). Development of a rational scale to assess the harm of drugs of potential misuse. *The Lancet*, 369(9566), pp. 1047–1053.

Nutt, D.J., King, L.A. and Phillips, L.D. (2010). Drug harms in the UK: A multicriteria decision analysis. *Lancet*, 376(9752), pp. 1558–1565.

Pawelz, J. (2017) Researching gangs: how to reach hard-to-reach populations and negotiate tricky issues in the field. *Forum: Qualitative Social Research*, 19(1).

Price, S. (2011) To what extent has recreational drug use become normalised amongst the student population at university? *Internet Journal of Criminology*.

Available at: https://958be75a-da42-4a45-aafa-549955018b18.filesusr. com/ugd/b93dd4_649323da70284e298816d88bf042790e.pdf [Accessed May 2021].

Punch, K. (2014) *Introduction to Social Research: Quantitative and Qualitative Approaches 3rd edn.* London: Sage.

Ralph, E. (2016) Constructing the perfect terrorist attack: critical evaluation of news values and media representations. *Internet Journal of Criminology.* Available at: https://958be75a-da42-4a45-aafa-549955018b18.filesusr. com/ugd/b93dd4_c4b66b3305624016a5be4f7935f160a8.pdf [Accessed May 2021].

Renzetti, C.M. and Lee, R.M. (1993) (Eds.) *Researching Sensitive Topics.* London: Sage.

Riffe, D., Lacy, S. and Fico, F. (1998) *Analyzing Media Messages: Using Quantitative Content Analysis in Research.* London: Routledge.

Rudestam, K.E. and Newton, R.R. (2015) *Surviving Your Dissertation A Comprehensive Guide To Content And Process.* London: Sage.

Scott, D. (2019) Western female jihad: how can understanding the motivations and roles of western Muslim women joining ISIS influence the UK's response?. *Internet Journal of Criminology.* Available at: https://958be75a-da42-4a45-aafa-549955018b18.filesusr.com/ugd/b93dd4_cbfeca9a5e8c4752b2acc69a70e71749.pdf [Accessed March 2021].

Shearman, G. (2021) An equal portrayal?: British media representations of male versus female child sex offenders. *Internet Journal of Criminology.* Available at: https://958be75a-da42-4a45-aafa-549955018b18.filesusr.com/ugd/9280ee_aad07010817348fcb6d70a168c42bb12.pdf [Accessed April 2021].

Smith, C.A. (2019) The uses of pilot studies in sociology: a processual understanding of preliminary research. *The American Sociologist* 50: 589–607.

Smith, K., Todd, M. and Waldman, J. (2009) *Doing your Undergraduate Social Science Dissertation.* London: Routledge.

Spiller, A.R. (2021) Knife crime in Medway, UK: the impact of media from a youth perspective. *Internet Journal of Criminology.* Available at: https://958be75a-da42-4a45-aafa-549955018b18.filesusr.com/ugd/9280ee_58a89f1baad349199697afcbaf42d520.pdf [Accessed August 2021].

Taherdoost, H. (2016) Sampling methods in research methodology; how to choose a sampling technique for research. *International Journal of Academic Research in Management.* 5(2), pp. 18–27.

Taylor, J. (2019) An empirical study of homelessness and crime. *Internet Journal of Criminology.* Available at: https://958be75a-da42-4a45-aafa-549955018b18.filesusr.com/ugd/b93dd4_783704224ff74f34a6922a8fa290b1ab.pdf [Accessed April 2021].

Toomey, E. (2019) An exploration of the understanding and perceptions of sexual consent among UCC final year criminology students. *Internet Journal of Criminology.* Available at: https://958be75a-da42-4a45-aafa-549955018b18.filesusr.com/ugd/b93dd4_308136b6d8a14c80a30ea3ff50c23998.pdf [Accessed March 2021].

Wahidin, A. and Moore, L. (2011) Ethics and criminological research. In: Davies, P., Francis, P. and Jupp, V. (Eds) *Doing Criminological Research* 2nd edn. London: Sage. pp. 287–307.

Walklate, S. (2007) Researching victims. In: King, R. and Wincup, E. (Eds) *Doing Research on Crime and Justice 2nd edn.* Oxford: Oxford University Press. pp. 315–342.

Wall, D.S. and Williams, M. (2011) Using the internet to research crime and justice. In: Davies, P., Francis, P. and Jupp, V. (Eds) *Doing Criminological Research 2nd edn.* London: Sage. pp. 262–280.

Walliman, N. (2006) *Social Research Methods.* London: Sage.

Walliman, N.S.R. (2014) *Your Undergraduate Dissertation: The Essential Guide for Success* 2nd edn. London: Sage.

Williams, K. (2014) *Getting Critical,* 2nd edn. Basingstoke: Palgrave.

Williams, M.J. (2017) Exploring students' attitudes towards various illicit substance use in relation to the UK drug classification system. *Internet Journal of Criminology.* Available at: https://958be75a-da42-4a45-aafa-549955018 b18.filesusr.com/ugd/b93dd4_34460b191d514a8598d50aa36660c59d.pdf [Accessed April 2021].

Wincup, E. (2017) *Criminological Research: Understanding Qualitative Methods* 2nd edn. London: Sage.

Index

Note: Page numbers in *italics* indicate figures and in **bold** indicate tables on the corresponding pages.

20–22, *21*; problematic criminology dissertation proposals in 16–18; types of research questions in 26, **27**
diary, dissertation 14–15
digital archives 71
Digital Panopticon 70
dissertation diary 14–15
dissertations, criminology: access and ethical issues with (*see* access and ethical issues); aims of 3–5; building on previous knowledge and/or methods 4; complexities of 8–9, **8–9**; demonstration of ideas through 4; designing (*see* design, criminology dissertation); empirical 7–8, 93–94, 103–108, **106**; examples of undergraduate 10–12, **12**; findings and discussions in (*see* findings and discussions); grounded in theory 7; as independent piece of work 3; library-based 7, 89–90, 100–103; literature reviews for (*see* literature reviews); methodology chapters in (*see* methodology chapters); originality in 4; preparing for 12–15; role of supervisor in 5–6, 39; stages of 1, **2**, 10, *11*; structuring of 115–120; types of 6–8; as validation of research 4; writing up and presenting (*see* writing up and presentation)

Economic and Social Research Council (ESRC) 67
empirical dissertations 7–8; findings and discussions in 103–108, **106**; methodology chapters in 93–94
ethics *see* access and ethical issues
examples of undergraduate dissertations 10–12, **12**
executive summaries 48
existing data *see* secondary data

findings and discussions: developing your academic voice and 98–100, **100**; distinctions between 103; in empirical projects 103–108, **106**; in library-based projects 100–103; qualitative 105–108, **106**; quantitative 104–105, 106–108
fluidity in writing 112

gaps in research, finding 21
Gillam, L. 32
Godfrey, B. 71
Google Scholar 48
government documents data 71–73
grabbing the readers' attention 113
Greetham, B. 4–5, 100
Guillemin, M. 32

harm avoidance 33
Harrop, A. R. 93–94, 107
Heap, V. 104
hedgers 99
Heslop, J. 89
Hill, J. 34
historical data **70**, 70–71
HMPPS National Research Committee 18
Home Office 61, 63

informed consent 34
Internet Journal of Criminology 10, 68
introductory chapters, writing up of 113–114
introductory materials for starting dissertations 12–13

Jacklin, A. 81
Jensen, E. A. 48
John Johnson Collection 70

King, R. D. 18

Laurie, C. 48
Lee, R. M. 37
LexisNexis 68
library-based dissertations 7; findings and discussions in 100–103; methodology chapters in 89–90
Liebling, A. 18
lists of acronyms 118
literature reviews: common questions on 56–57; conclusion to 54–56; defined 42–43; devising search terms for 45–46, *46*; effective

For Product Safety Concerns and Information please contact our EU
representative GPSR@taylorandfrancis.com
Taylor & Francis Verlag GmbH, Kaufingerstraße 24, 80331 München, Germany

www.ingramcontent.com/pod-product-compliance
Lightning Source LLC
Chambersburg PA
CBHW050531270326
41926CB00015B/3163

9780367859992